The Jena Campaign: 1806

The Jena Campaign: 1806

The Twin Battles of Jena & Auerstadt
Between Napoleon's French and
the Prussian Army

F. N. Maude

LEONAUR

The Jena Campaign: 1806—The Twin Battles of Jena & Auerstadt
Between Napoleon's French and the Prussian Army
by F. N. Maude

Published by Leonaur Ltd

ISBN: 978-1-84677-235-1 (hardcover)
ISBN: 978-1-84677-236-8 (softcover)

http://www.leonaur.com

Publisher's Notes

The opinions expressed in this book are those of the author
and are not necessarily those of the publisher.

Contents

Maps   7

Introduction   19

The Prussian Army Before Jena   27

The French Army Before Jena   48

Prussian Movements to October 13th   66

French Movements to October 13th   108

The Battles of Jena & Auerstadt   141

Conclusion & Comments   167

Maps

Positions on Evening of 11th October

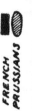

FRENCH
PRUSSIANS

LEIPZIG

ALTENBURG

MERSEBURG

WEISSENFELS

Molsen

Teuchern

Münowen

Pegau

ZEITZ

CAV.

ELSTER

Grossen

Laucha

UNSTRUT R.

Freiburg

Stössen

Eisenberg

SCALE —
12 MILES = 1 INCH.

1
760.320

Bibra

NAUMBURG
Kösen

Crossburg

Dornburg

Bürgel

Eckardtsberge

Hassenhausen

Auerstädt

SULZA

ILM R.

Apolda

Zweizen

HOHENLOHE

Buttstädt

Buttelstedt

WEIMAR

Erfurth

ILM R.

Mellbager

ILM R.

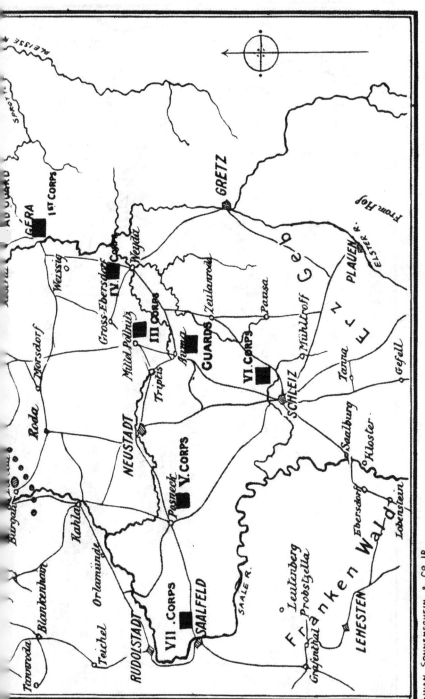

Positions Night of 13th October

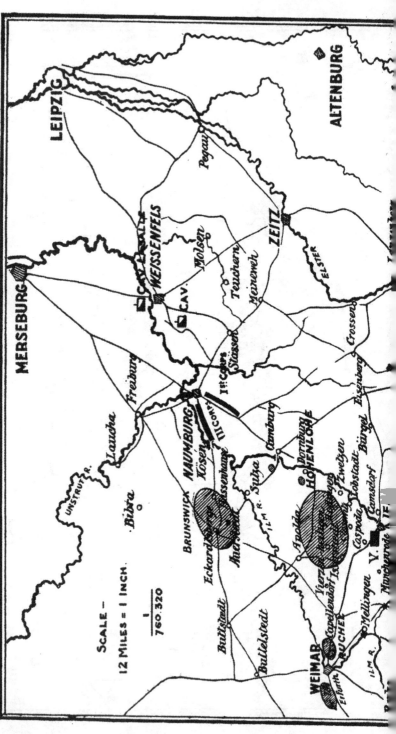

FRENCH ■
PRUSSIANS ◨

SCALE —
12 MILES = 1 INCH.

$$\frac{1}{760.320}$$

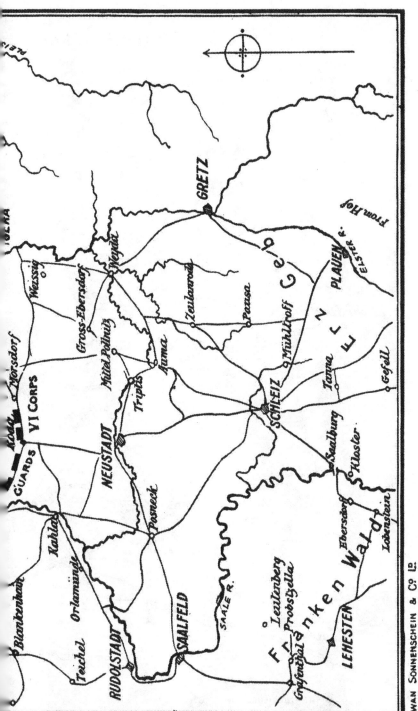

SWAN SONNENSCHEIN & C? L?

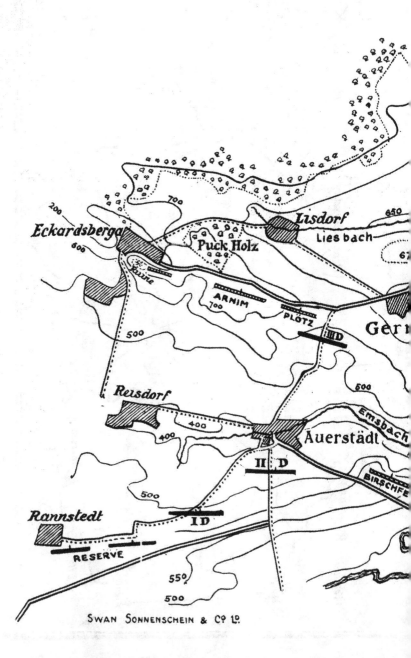

SWAN SONNENSCHEIN & C^O L^D.

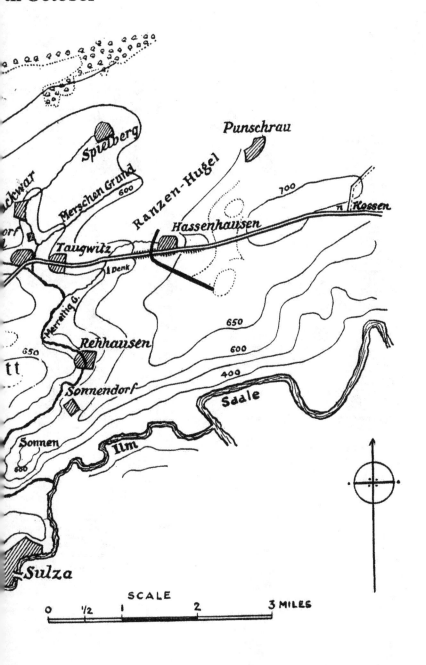

Punschrau

Spielberg

Merschen Grund

Ranzen-Hügel

Hassenhausen

700

Rossen

600

Taugwitz

Denk

Merretig G.

650

600

Rehhausen

650

400

Sonnendorf

Saale

t t

Sonnen

Ilm

Sulza

SCALE

0   ½   1   2   3 MILES

Situation About 1 o'clock

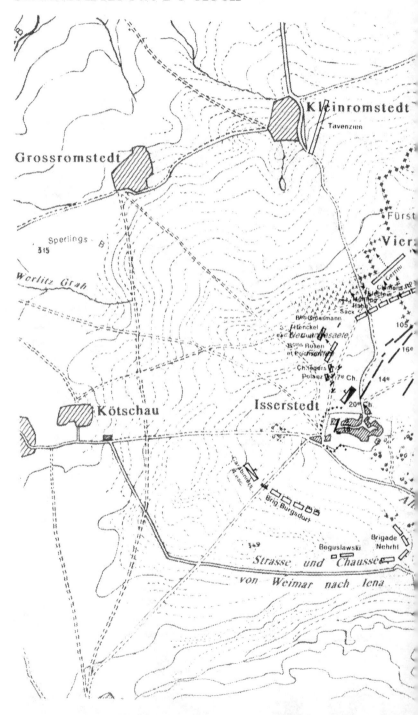

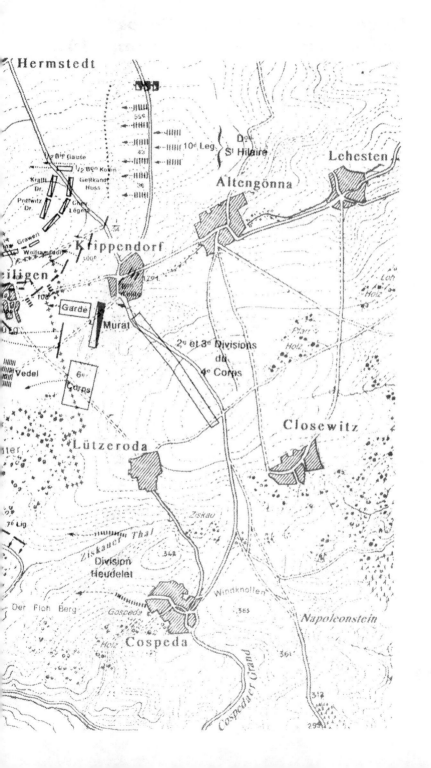

Engagement of the 5th Corps
and Tauenzien 14th Oct. 6 am --10 am

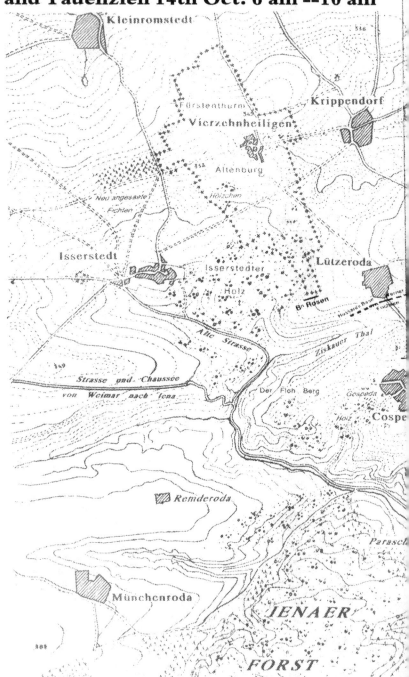

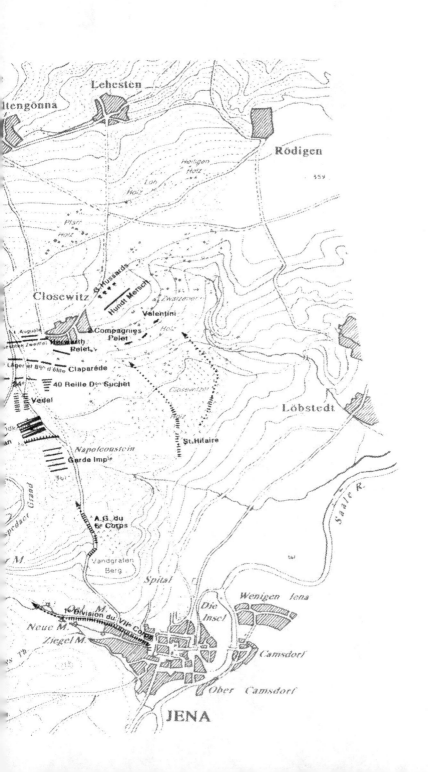

Introduction
(Written in 1909)

There is no battle in modern history which has exerted so profound an influence on the progress of humanity as that fought out upon the plains overlooking Jena on October 14, 1806.

Here the old and the new school, absolute Monarchy and Democracy, both in their highest form of embodiment, met one another under fairly equal conditions, and as a consequence all Europe now stands as a series of armed camps, and even in far Japan and China, the dread of War and all that the word implies, is compelling men to undergo a training in truth, honour and self-denial which bids fair to prepare the field for a harvest of ethical fruits; a development far more wide-reaching than any dogmatic revelation has as yet attained.

This is all in the order of evolution. In the beginning, mankind had to learn in the hard school of experience the iron law of the "pack," the curbing of the selfish instinct of self-preservation; then had to come the training of the intellect by the spread of book-learning and education which loosened the law of blind instinct; and now follows the training of the "Will of the individual," to restrain the mind and to teach it how to apply its powers for the greatest good of our common humanity.

Left to itself, intellect threatened the foundation of all society, for alone it cannot prove the existence of any object better worth living for than "self." The survival of the fittest is its last word, and since nothing more than our existence in this life can be intellectually demonstrated, socialism and anarchy, ultimately the rule of the "super-man," was all that intellect had to hold out to us, and the unrestrained cult of this tyranny results in loss of sanity, not seldom in dangerous madness. But from this fate, the necessity which compels nearly two-thirds of the male inhabitants of Europe to submit to a systematic training of the Will, bids fair to save us; for through the Will and by its exercise, the individual is prepared to receive the knowledge of higher laws than those, the truth of which can be intellectually demonstrated. It may be that very few are as yet ripe to receive such knowledge or to be entrusted with the power it confers, but already it is quite evident to those with eyes to see, that the military training of the past century is humanizing whole populations in the most marked degree, and is proving, in those countries which have embraced it the most thoroughly—whether as volunteers, or by the compulsion of their own law—a, source of material prosperity and general comfort far beyond anything which the ordinary laws of supply and demand could have enabled the thinker to predict.

In the period prior to the French Revolution, the relation between Kings and their people were briefly these. Apart from any question of duty on either side, it was to the direct personal interest of the King to obtain for his people the best possible conditions for developing their own resources, either by the conquest of fresh countries with which they could trade unrestrictedly, or by specialization of their several functions of trade, manufactures, agriculture, defence, and so forth. The more perfectly each of these worked, the more rapidly wealth accumulated, and the more taxes could be paid, which naturally enhanced the position of the King. Where the King possessed executive ability, and chose a sound Executive Committee, the system succeeded well, as the many public works, roads and canals executed in France during the reign of Louis XIV abundantly prove.

It was to no one's interest to oppress the people, but the system needed constant watchfulness and intense centralization; it was, in fact, exactly like the discipline of an Army concentrated on a small area, where every unit is within immediate contact with the General's Headquarters.

In an Army in immediate contact with its enemy, no one objects to the curtailment of personal liberty, which instant readiness for action entails, and more or less, every one agrees cheerfully to the specialization of functions between the several grades, and the several arms, etc., that efficiency obviously requires. When the enemy possesses the craft and cruelty of the Red Indian, and the stake and torture are the penalty for lack of watchfulness and consequent defeat, it is the men, not the Commanders, who settle the scale of punishment for offences which endanger their security, and since (during generations of chronic warfare before awakening humanitarianism had placed any limit to the atrocities invading hosts felt themselves at liberty to inflict) the civil populations of Europe had grown up under closely analogous conditions, they willingly learnt to submit themselves to the iron code of Law, and to the punishments needed to unite them all for the common good. But when after the horrors of the Thirty Years' War, a reaction against the barbarism which had characterized that struggle set in, and prolonged periods of prosperity began to intervene in the hitherto unbroken monotony of the National struggles for existence, the powers conceded to the King for punishment of offences against the common good began to be considered excessive. People began to resent enforced submission to the law, and especially to the existence of a King as representative of that law.

The same causes were at work all over Europe, and are indeed still in operation even now, but whereas during the eighteenth century France enjoyed an almost uninterrupted freedom from serious invasion, and had the advantage of a rich soil and an admirable climate, Prussia and Austria were the scenes of many and great conflicts which strained their resources to the utmost. Thus the forces which form the sanction of the old feudal system were kept at a far higher tension than could be maintained in France.

Moreover, whilst Prussia had the good fortune to be ruled by one of the greatest soldiers and administrators of all time, Frederick the Great, France was afflicted by a series of incompetent monarchs, who by the choice of inferior instruments made the burden of the law fall with unendurable heaviness upon the shoulders of the people.

It was not the "Law" which was bad in itself, but the corruption of the agents through which it was administered, and as the people in France no longer felt or saw the absolute necessity for its unreformed continuance, a passion for reform invaded all classes from nobles to peasants, and the agents of the. Law proved powerless to enforce it.

It was not the lower classes which revolted, but the upper ones who broke down the barriers and enabled the crowd to pass them.

The same process was at work in all other kingdoms of the European continent, but the level of intelligence in France being markedly higher, and the concentration of people in towns and the means of communication between them being materially greater, it was possible for the "crowds" to combine and to develop a "thought-wave" which turned for the time being the individuals of these several crowds into dangerous maniacs.

As Gustave le Bon in his *Psychologie des Foules* has pointed out, the principal agents in the successive waves of terror that swept over France were, under normal conditions, quite normal and peaceable citizens indistinguishable from the mass by either intellect, ability, or force of character. After the strain of the Revolution relaxed, those who survived sank back into the obscurity from which they had so phenomenally emerged, bearing thereafter for the most part no trace of the responsibility they had incurred for the hideous crimes against humanity in which they had played the leading roles. They had been, in fact, merely irresponsible agents of the National Will, and their type existed in every other country, only the conditions for focussing the national thought-power upon them were not yet in existence, and the irony of events determined that when at length the progress of the French Revolution created in other countries the necessary conditions, the outrages against humanity of which the Revolution had been guilty, focussed the national thought-power upon defence, and not upon internal reform.

The ruling Princes of Europe were fully alive to the existence of the revolutionary ferment amongst their own people when the French Revolution broke out, but they were not psychologists enough to foresee the inevitable consequence which must follow their direct interference in the affairs of that Nation. This was to unite all parties in France against them and to weld these parties into a homogeneous Nation capable of efforts beyond the calculations of Statesmen accustomed only to the normal conditions of the existing monarchical constitutions in which a firmly administered "Law" determined with accuracy the fighting output of the machine.

The appearance of the Armies of the Coalition on French soil had the same effect as the interference of a third party in a family feud. The French did not exactly "fly to arms," but each Frenchman flew to the conviction that his neighbour ought to die for his country, and with this unanimity behind them, the Legislative Councils, no matter how temporary might be their existence, found no difficulty in promulgating and enforcing decrees which truly embodied the National Will.

Thus the veteran Generals of Europe faced an absolutely unparalleled problem, for never before in history had such a force been called into being.

Scharnhorst was the first to appreciate the full consequences of this new departure, and his short pamphlet, *Ueber die Ur-*

sachen unsere Niederlagen in den Niederlanden, published in 1794, should form the starting point of any attempt to unravel the occurrences of the subsequent twenty years. But his prescience was not shared by others of his time, and nothing in the tactical incidents of the early years of the struggle really justified mistrust in the time-honoured methods and principles of the Prussian Army (as indeed our own success with the same methods sufficiently demonstrates). It was only when the Emperor Napoleon had succeeded in alienating the Will of his people, and the French by their exactions had created the same force of "National Will" amongst the peoples they had successively overrun, that the scales were turned and it became possible for the representatives of the monarchical principle to drive relatively untrained men to the slaughter with the same ruthlessness that the French Revolutionary Leaders had employed.

Our present danger results from the fact that this need of national unanimity against an enemy has never yet been driven home to us in England. We have fought relatively with weapons of tempered steel and have still to realize that men can be killed by the bludgeon as well as by the rapier. Hence we are for ever clamouring for unattainable perfection and losing sight of the fact that men will always be forthcoming to fight if only the Will of the Nation is there to drive them onward; and the expression "Nation" includes both women and children.

I do not of course contest the value of trained, disciplined and organized troops (what soldier ever would?), but I do most earnestly deprecate the attitude of those who believe calamity inevitable, because we cannot yet turn out Divisions equipped and ready down to the last gaiter button.

Napoleon preferred to have his soldiers well shod and well fed, but when the occasion required it he knew how to make them fight bare-footed, in rags, and hungry, and our own records are there to show that our men have often endured the same desperate privations. If it be argued that they were old and tried regiments that have done so, the answer is, that though the regiments were old, as a fact the bulk of the men have generally been exceedingly young, and very indifferently trained. It is the age-long traditions of the various corps that tells, far more than the percentage of recruits in the ranks. By putting our souls into the work of the County Associations and helping them to bind the ties between the regular battalions and the territorials yet closer (the beginning has long since been made), we shall be forging that spirit of unanimity in the Nation without which modern strategical and tactical methods are impracticable, *which is all the more formidable when it is the voluntary expression of a nation's growth, and not the compulsory creation of its fears.*

That we shall be tried before many years are passed, though not perhaps in the form it is the fashion to believe, admits of very little doubt. When once the pursuit of wealth and the cult of self exceeds a certain limit, natural Law steps in to redress the balance, and War, Pestilence and Famine are her executive agents. That we shall collapse under the strain nothing in our recent history leads me to admit. Indeed, from the activity of the peace party I draw my greatest hopes, for this very activity proves the exceeding slowness of our race to change its fighting spirit for the calm of pusillanimity. These people still believe that the profession of the soldier is merely to kill for killing's sake, and imagine War to be the mere butcher's work of the early Anglo-Saxons, when great physical strength and an irritable liver ("Berserker fury" it was called) were all the qualifications needed to excel in it. If they were right I should be the first to join their ranks. But bring it home to them that the modern training for War not only needs, but actually turns out, men of such self-control that they can not only look death in the face unflinching, but actually keep the strongest passions of human nature in subjection (as they actually did in the Afghan War of 1878, and the recent South African Campaigns), and furthermore that the essence of a soldier's contract *is willingness to die, not the desire to kill,* then when danger threatens, they will be as ready to come to the ranks as their ancestors were in the days of Cromwell. Even if their untrained arms are not of much immediate service, the tenacity of their characters will be a valuable asset of the national wealth.

Meanwhile, let those of us who really are in earnest in our common service, remember Nelson's signal before Trafalgar, and let each of us attend to *"his duty,"* not everybody else's "duty." That "duty" now is loyally to support the existing Law, and not like troublesome children to quarrel with established facts and refuse to play, because they are not allowed to cram their several hobbies down other people's throats.

F. N. Maude
February 22nd, 1909

Chapter 1

The Prussian Army Before Jena

Up to the outbreak of the French Revolution, the Western Armies of Europe had developed on almost parallel lines, though each bore more or less the imprint of its topographical surroundings.

All these had evolved from the old feudal idea of liability for military service, by all able-bodied men, to their Overlord in return for his protection; but in practice the people had very generally commuted their personal service for money payments, and mercenary standing Armies stood everywhere ready to bear the first brunt of the enemy's onset. Only in the last resort was recourse had to the original militia levy, and then the men, taken by lot or other compulsion, were usually drafted into existing units of the standing Army to replace its losses.

Within these standing Armies there was little national spirit; essentially the men contracted to give their services to the Monarch in return for pay and other specified advantages, and if the contract was not punctually kept, they felt little compunction in taking service under a better paymaster.

Particularly was this the case with the officers, and these birds of passage tended largely to spread a general knowledge of contemporary military thought throughout all Armies, thus bringing them all to a general level of efficiency in practice; but the topographical surroundings still asserted their influence, and gradually each Army differentiated itself in its spirit—if not in its forms—from its neighbours. Thus, though at the close of the Wars in the Netherlands, all Armies alike had discovered that every musket in the fighting line was the first condition of victory and therefore fought fundamentally in "line," the Prussians, accustomed to train in an almost level country, paid far greater attention to accuracy of movement than either the French or Austrians, whose far more varied experience had taught them that more elastic methods were often essential.

Fundamentally, the idea which underlay the Prussian tactics was the same as that which for years had controlled the British Navy. The weight of metal thrown per unit of time was decisive—the question of accuracy of fire was got over by closing with the enemy until it seemed physically impossible for a bullet to miss—and in open ground it seems that occasionally this ideal was realized. Thus at the Battle of Crefeld, it is said that the first Prussian volley, stretched out 75 per cent, of the enemy, and like the "perfect volley" of Quebec practically decided the day.[1]

But the difficult manoeuvres in "Line" necessary to carry out this ideal exposed the troops during their performance to great dangers from the enemy's Cavalry and skirmishers, hence Cavalry superiority was the primary condition of success. As throughout the Wars of Frederick the Great—Mollwitz only excepted—this superiority was incontestably on the Prussian side, they were able to manoeuvre with a freedom impossible to other Armies; hence, since the Infantry formed the larger proportion of the whole Army, the Prussian victories began to be assigned by tradition to the excellent manoeuvring power of the Infantry, and not primarily to the undisputed efficiency of the Cavalry, which alone provided the conditions that rendered this manoeuvring possible.

---

1. See also the first volley of the Guards at Fontenoy, said to have brought down 690 French, practically the whole battalion.

But though public opinion, always on the side of the victors, generally endorsed this conclusion, and after the Seven Years' War made the Prussian Infantry the model for all Europe, there were still some men left in the French Army—not without weight—who, remembering their experiences at Roszbach, declined to accept this popular superstition. The divergence between French and Prussian practice which finally led to the disaster of Jena (the after-effects of which have not even yet disappeared) takes its origin from that celebrated field, where within forty-five minutes—more or less—Seydlitz with his 33 squadrons, backed up only by 18 guns and 7 battalions, swept away the Allied forces under Soubise, some 60,000 strong, killed, wounded and captured some 10,000 of them and brought in 21 standards and 72 guns.[1]

To understand the real difference between the two Armies which met on that fateful morning of October 14,1806, it is necessary first to form a clear mental image of the typical Prussian recruit of Frederick the Great's epoch. Almost invariably he came direct from the plough's tail, and was more densely stupid than it is easy for any one in the twentieth century to conceive. He was clumsy, loutish and ungainly, even as our own yokels were half a century ago, and as a kind of standard by which to gauge his stupidity, Prince Hohenlohe gives us some anecdotes in his *Letters on Infantry*, describing the recruits with which he had to deal in the Artillery of the Guard during the fifties—relatively picked men—which must seem almost incredible to those who have never seen the men as I used to do when a boy at school in Germany.

If this was the type of country recruit after the schoolmaster had been abroad in the land, with compulsion to back him, for nearly thirty years, it may be imagined what they were like fifty years before his advent, yet these were the men

---

1. See Pruss. Off. *Seven Years' War,* vol. v, pp. 220, *et seq.,* also von der Goltz, *Boszbach und Jena.* Only 7 battalions of the 27 available were engaged; of these 2 fired 7 rounds each, 5 only 2 rounds each.

who, somehow or other, had to be licked into such shape that they could march steadily in line across country, keeping the touch of the elbow so exactly, without jostling or overcrowding, that at the word "Halt" each man had just room, and no more, to go through the exceedingly complicated movements necessary to load his musket at the rate of five to six loads per minute, notwithstanding the confusion created by the enemy's fire.

The intensity of this fire which had to be faced seems hardly to be realized. Because the regulations of all Armies laid down 200 yards or paces as the limit of effective fire, it has been very generally assumed that effective fire was synonymous with the extreme range of the weapon, and that troops never made use of their fire power except at these limited ranges. Actually troops got out of hand even as they do nowadays, and once the fire was started, fired as high and as wildly as they do still when excited.

Hence (since at extreme elevation the musket carried about 1,200 paces) the front of a position was thoroughly swept by round shot, case and musket bullets for a good 1,000 yards from the muzzles, and through this rain of death the Infantry had to move stolidly forward, not returning a shot until the order was given. More can not be demanded of them even at the present day.

The comparison will be clearer if we take a specific instance, and calculate the approximate number of bullets delivered by the defender per 1,000 yards of front.

At the Battle of Prague, May 6, 1757, Frederick the Great planned a great outflanking manoeuvre, but his intention was anticipated by the Austrians, who formed a fresh front to meet it, and occupied a position on the summit of along glacis-like slope some 1,000 yards in extent, up which the Prussians had to advance, like their descendants of the Prussian Guards at St. Privat, August 18, 1870; but of the two, the glacis at Prague offered the least cover.

On a front of 2,500 yards the Austrians deployed 38 heavy guns, and 10 battalions, the latter standing three deep, and firing about three rounds a minute.

The batteries opened fire the moment the Prussians came within range, first with round shot, then with grape, which ricocheted along up to 800 yards, finally changing to case, and the Infantry very soon chimed in, though the precise moment can no longer be fixed. But as the excitement increased it may be assumed that the whole 1,200 yards slope was swept with a fairly uniform shower of bullets through which the second line had to make its way without a chance of returning their enemy's fire.

The total number of bullets from this front which would strike the ground somewhere within that 1,200 yards and with sufficient remaining velocity to disable a man in every minute would be about 100,000.

Now, under modern conditions, 2,500 Infantry on the same front would deliver about 50,000 bullets a minute, and these bullets would fall under equal conditions of unsteadiness somewhere over an area about 5,000 yards deep, so that the number of bullets falling on each unit of surface would only be one eighth as great. Actually the Prussian battalions were torn to pieces; several losing over 50 per cent, of their men, whereas 5 per cent, nowadays appears to be considered a butchery.[1]

Nothing could bring out in more striking fashion the difference between the demands made then and now upon the discipline of the men, or explain more clearly the reason of

---

1. The point is this—owing to the short range of the musket in 1757 every bullet had to reach the ground somewhere within the 1,200 yard limit, no matter at what angle it might have been discharged; with the modern rifle very many would travel 5,000 yards. In 1757 it was beyond the power of artillery to seriously unsteady the aim of the defenders' infantry; nowadays the guns can so shroud the front of their enemy in dust and smoke that he can no longer see a target to aim at, and in proportion as the gunners make more or less use of their power, the density of the opposing fire is diminished till it approximates to a uniform distribution—like rain which falls equally on the just and unjust alike.

the extreme importance war-experienced soldiers attached to the drill-ground in those days. They knew perfectly well that in the excitement of action, the minute prescriptions of the drill-ground could not be observed, but they knew also that unless the men were trained until the idea of going forward, and the motions of loading and firing, had become almost automatic habit, they could not be induced to face the fire at all.

History shows the old drill-masters to have been right, for whereas the well-drilled troops of Frederick the Great bore victoriously losses as heavy as even 60 per cent, in individual cases, and carried position after position with not more than 15,000 men to the mile, British troops, in fact, often got through with even less than 10,000, the hastily-trained levies of the French Revolution rarely stood up to more than 10 per cent, of loss, and ultimately Napoleon could only succeed in his attacks with men crowded together at the rate of 100,000 to the mile, and then only as a consequence of his superior Artillery preparation.

The two ideas were fundamentally different, and this difference must be grasped if the lessons of the Jena campaign are to be understood. The essence of Frederick's Line tactics was to economize the lives of his soldiers, *that of Napoleon was to economize the drain on the State by curtailing the duration of the whole campaign.* The campaign of Jena lasted seven days; Frederick's Great War lasted seven years. This is not purely an invidious comparison. Both systems were the necessary outcome of the social conditions—using the term in its widest sense—of the times, and neither could conceivably have copied the method of the other. *The fault which wrecked Prussia was that her rulers failed to interpret the signs of their times,* and relied on methods which had become atrophied through disuse.

The cause is not far to seek. The French Army had grown up and adapted itself to its work by contact with the actual hard facts of War. The Prussian rulers were soldiers only and not Statesmen, hence they failed to perceive how profoundly the whole nature of War had been influenced by the growth of the spirit of nationality which found its expression in the Armies of the French Revolution.

The Seven Years' War had been fought and its battles won for the Prussians by highly-specialized workmen, duly and thoroughly trained for their trade, and the hopeless poverty into which that colossal struggle had plunged the whole Nation formed in itself the best reason for perpetuating the old system. Specialized labour being wanted in every trade, it paid better to leave the peasant and artisan in their homes, and to hire wastrels from adjacent countries, in which (they having escaped the ravages of war) labour was cheaper and more abundant. There were also numbers of other restless characters (who hated the settled life of the towns, and were attracted by the prospects of change which a soldier's life seemed to hold out to them, the usual class from which recruits have always been drawn to voluntary Armies) available within the country itself, if not within their own districts, and with these it was possible to form the cadres of a standing Army capable of great expansion by partially trained men drawn from the immediate vicinity of the regimental headquarters, voluntarily if possible, but by the ballot as a last resort.

The country was divided into regimental districts called "cantons," each administered by what was practically a "County Association," pledged by law to provide and equip so many battalions, and left to themselves to find the men as best they could, with recourse to the ballot if necessary. In agricultural districts, the periods of training being adjusted to harvest requirements, as a rule no difficulty was found in providing troops enough to bring the battalions up to a war strength by men who engaged for what was practically life service. Indeed, most regiments always had a small supernumerary list of waiting men called "Krümpers" as a first reserve to replace casualties. But in the towns where trade was brisk, so much difficulty was experienced in finding men at all, that they frequently petitioned, and often successfully, to commute their liability to provide men by a money payment to the War budget, from which sum the State defrayed the cost of attracting recruits from "foreign," i.e., extra territorial countries, generally Germans. No doubt far too many of these men had left their homes from considerations of expediency, not of enthusiasm for the Prussian cause, yet arriving singly at headquarters, they were easily assimilated by their regiments, and ultimately did much to break down the feeling of parochialism that for so long impeded the realization of German Unity, which in its present form owes far more to the lessons in duty and patriotism learnt under the colours of Frederick the Great's battalions, than modern historians have ever acknowledged.

During the years immediately succeeding the great campaigns, life under the Prussian colours was by no means unattractive. The discipline was not more severe than in all other Armies of the period, certainly not more so than in ours, and the whole Nation, being still grateful to their defenders, whose services had been so devoted that none would dare to cavil at them, showed the men much hospitality and friendliness. But the country recovered so rapidly from the ravages of the War—*agricultural communities invariably do*—that the people soon forgot the debt they owed to the Army, and resented its existence as a tax on their further prosperity. As trade and industry offered higher rewards, it became more and more difficult to find recruits of good standing, thus the Army lost in social consideration. But as the men in their handsome uniforms, and with their better carriage and manners, preserved all their attractiveness for the women, the civilians grew jealous of them, and as usual accused them of seducing their wives and daughters.

That a certain number of hard cases did occur cannot of course be doubted; as long as there are men and women in the world such things will always happen, but their frequency was not sufficient to justify the restrictions on the soldier's liberty that the civilians demanded and obtained, which, thanks to the power of identification and discipline possessed by the military authorities ended by turning the barracks into a prison-house and the soldier into a ticket-of-leave man.[1]

The fact that a number of drilled soldiers were allowed by law to practise a trade within their garrisons, and thanks to their habits of discipline and concentration usually throve where the civilian failed—still further accentuated the strained relations between the two classes, and when the ferment of French Revolutionary doctrines reached the great industrial centres, it can be imagined how rapidly the contagion spread. We who have lived through something of the same kind in England before the short service system and the Volunteers began to break down the barriers between the Nation and the Army can easily picture the situation, for there was no complaint made against the soldier and his calling, his morals and his vices, which cannot be paralleled from our own experience in recent years. Indeed, in some quarters where the doctrines of the Manchester "peace with dishonour" school are still held in reverence—more numerous, I fear, than many will believe—the same wild accusations are still flung broadcast by the Press, precisely as in Prussia in the days before the great catastrophe.

Gradually, under pressure of these many conflicting tendencies, the composition of the Army had been settled on a basis of approximately one-third of "Foreigners" to two-thirds of natives of each district; about four-fifths of the latter

---

1. Up to the period of 1806 every Prussian burgher had the right to stop a soldier found a mile away from his camp or quarters, and demand to see his pass. If the pass was not in order the soldier had to accompany the civilian to the nearest guard where he was made a prisoner. If a man was missed at any roll call, a gun was fired from the barracks or a bell rung, announcing the fact to the whole countryside, (as is still the case at our convict prisons,) and every one was free to hunt down the wretched absentee.

being called up for six weeks' training annually, and sent on furlough, or allowed to work at their trades, sleeping in barracks, for the remainder of the year.

Practically the strength under arms was fixed by the rule that the soldier should have three nights in bed for one on guard, and as the guard duties were heavy, the above proportion was generally arrived at. It speaks volumes for the tact and efficiency of both officers and non-commissioned officers, on whom in the latter years the work of drilling the men principally fell, that in spite of this short service of only six weeks, the drill-ground training of the men, as evinced in the great spring and autumn reviews, remained to the last the wonder of all Europe, and did not fail them even on the field of Jena itself.

The whole of the Army was under the direction of the "Ober Kriegs Collegium," a body of the highest experts, to whom the King stood in the same relation as our Secretary of State for War holds to the Army Council, with this difference, that whereas the British Secretary of State is generally a civilian and responsible to a Parliament almost devoid of military experience, the King of Prussia was always a trained soldier, theoretically responsible to himself alone, though in practice he had not really as much actual control over the almost automatic working of his own treasury as Parliament can exercise upon our national purse-strings. In plain homely English, "it would have been more than his place was worth" to impose fresh taxation in the existing ferment of public opinion. He could only wait until the general rise of prosperity brought with it an increase of revenue due to the extinction of debt charges. This was as much an axiom of the Prussian Treasury as it is still in England, but as events were soon to show, it proved a most futile financial policy in the end.

The "Ober Kriegs Collegium" recognized fully the needs of many and far-reaching reforms, and countless proposals for the establishment of an improved militia and for universal service reached it from all sources, which were all duly circulated and commented on, often most ably. But there was no driving power of public opinion behind them to secure the necessary funds, and in fairness to their memory it must be remembered that with Napoleon knocking at their door, it was no time "to swap horses," and no far-reaching reform, however sound in principle, could have borne fruit enough to justify the experiment in the few years which elapsed before the storm burst upon them. There can be no getting away from the essential fact, *viz.*, that Prussia, with a population of barely 10,000,000, could not stand up single-handed to France with 36,000,000, for an indefinite period of time. Her fundamental mistake lay in not realising this from the first, and guiding her policy to secure honourable Allies.

Under the circumstances the Kriegs Collegium did the best they could to meet the spirit of their times, by re-arranging existing units in imitation of the fashions of the day. The French having introduced Army Corps—complete little Armies each with their Cavalry, Artillery and Infantry—the same idea was applied by the Prussians to their Divisions. The great mass of magnificent Cavalry, which under Seydlitz had won such immortal renown, was split up into groups and allotted to the several Infantry Commands, who not understanding the true spirit of the Arm, were incapable of inspecting it, and thus keeping it up to its former standard.

The Infantry had their share of guns—battalion guns already, but the Commission failed to distinguish between the extra efficiency of the battery unit, and the six guns divided up amongst three battalions—so the battalion guns, light six pounders, remained, and were reinforced by batteries of heavier pieces, 12 and 18 pounders, with 4½ inch howitzers taken from the "Artillery Reserve" which Frederick the Great had built up with the express intention of using it in the Napoleonic manner. The Infantry Divisions were further subdivided into Brigades, Regiments and Battalions, but the Regiment was the highest existing unit in peace, and the Staff Officers intended to ensure the harmonious working of the whole, though individually highly educated, had enjoyed no previous opportunities of working with their units in manoeuvres, but had at most assisted to handle them in the spring and autumn reviews, which took place from standing camps, or barracks, and were really "battle drills," not manoeuvres in the modern sense at all.

So much for the combined units. Taking the arms in detail we find that it was the Cavalry which had suffered most from the prevailing mania for economy. This is always and everywhere the case, for the horse cannot actively resent the suppression of his rations. He can only passively fall off in condition, and if external condition is the principal criterion of efficiency, his scale of work is reduced until by heated stables and foul air sufficient appearance of sleekness is attained to deceive the untrained eye.

This means the suppression of the "gallop" altogether and the use of the "trot" only for limited periods, and when after twenty to thirty years young subalterns have risen to command—who have never, or rarely, seen the whole regiment gallop—they do not care to take the responsibility of trying the experiment.

But with this elimination of the faster paces, there followed a very decided lowering of the standard of equitation demanded from the individual man, and since as soon as he was passed as efficient he could be allowed to go on furlough, and his pay be saved for the squadron chest, the men spent less and less time with the colours, till as Marwitz has proved to us in his *Diary*, a troop of 66 privates could only have 7 well-trained riders, whilst of the remainder, 33, were on furlough, and only mounted their horses 35 times in the year; 10 were "Freiwachter" and rode even less, and 16 were still doing recruit training.

As a set-off to all these disadvantages it is probable that the horses sent out to work on the farms developed much better condition from the fresh air and exercise, but for the most part they seem to have been entirely grass fed.

It is, however, a certainty that not a single squadron in the Prussian Cavalry that took the field in 1806 could have come up to the great King's requirements of 1754, when he sent the celebrated Baireuth Dragoons, the heroes of Hohenfriedberg, to three months extra drill for failing to reach his standard at the Camp at Neisse.[1]

The Artillery as an Arm is even more difficult to reconstruct for the papers bearing on the subject are promised by the Prussian General Staff; but have not yet appeared. Briefly, they had hardly yet differentiated out into "Field" and "Siege," though the idea of Horse Artillery was in the air, having, in fact, been already tested during the Seven Years' War, and the nucleus of the future light and mobile field Artillery existed in the battalion guns. None of the batteries appear to have been kept horsed in peace, whilst the drivers, though they did not march past on foot in smock frocks with waggoners' whips like the Royal Artillery at Woolwich in 1792 (see Duncan's *History of the Royal Regiment of Artillery*, p. 192), seem to have had no practical training in horsemanship at all, and their horses were taken straight from the plough.

The battalion guns were manned by a crew of eight men apiece who were enlisted as "Carpenters," the originals of the regimental Pioneers. From time to time they were inspected by Officers of the Artillery and sent to the Artillery School for practice. Their chief point appears to have been celerity in loading, and as a rule they could get off 10 rounds of case in the minute, which at roughly 100 bullets to the round gave 600, or the same fire power relatively to the Infantry as the

---

1. See *Cavalry, its Past and Future,* by the author.

modern maxim or other machine gun. But they could also fire both grape and round shot, which latter, with ricochet practice, was effective up to 2,000 yards.

In action these guns were dragged by their own detachments which limited their weight to about 24 cwt. inclusive (8 cwt. gun, 8 cwt. carriage; about 8 cwt. for limber), and on the march they had four horses harnessed tandem fashion, and carried in their limbers 30 rounds of shot, and 30 of case. A further supply followed them in a six-horse cart.

The great drawback to the whole Arm was that it was in no sense an *Arme d'élite* as in France. Its officers were looked down upon as socially inferior both to the Cavalry and Infantry, and the master-gunners and quartermasters seem to have been both careless in the maintenance of their stores, and not above suspicion with regard to contracts. Fortunately, many of the resulting deficiencies were revealed in the mobilization of 1805 and put right in consequence.

Of the Engineers, it is unnecessary to speak. They were almost exclusively trained for fortress duties and took no part in the decisive events of the War. Like the Artillery, the officers were held as ineligible for higher commands, a fact which, when reported to Napoleon after Jena, drew from him the criticism, *"c'est bien bête."*

It has been about the training and tactics of the Infantry, however, that discussion has principally turned, and for seventy years the verdict of posterity has been almost unanimous in its condemnation of all pre-Jena methods. Even nowadays, although the opening up of the Archives of the War Ministry in Berlin has done much to remove the many misconceptions surrounding the whole period, nevertheless the prejudice with which the subject is regarded is still very strong, and most writers feel compelled to deal with the matter in an apologetic tone for the wisdom of their forefathers, where in fact no apology whatever is needed. On the contrary, both other contemporary and also more recent experience has shown that the said forefathers knew more of the psychology of War—as from their far longer experience might *à priori* have been anticipated—than their present day descendants.

It is now clearly established that in all essentials the training and tactical methods of the old pre-Jena period—i.e., from 1800 to 1806—was identical in spirit with those in use in the British Army at the same date and for many subsequent years, and our ample experience in the Peninsula, at Waterloo, and in India, is there as sufficient justification both for ourselves and the Prussians.

In so far as departures in principle—not in detail—from these methods which have arisen of late years, are capable of scientific justification, these are due exclusively to changes in strategic methods, and alterations in the balance of power of the three Arms, together with the fundamental difference in the raising of Armies, which has rendered the life of the individual trained soldier no longer a matter of such great relative importance to the State. It is not of much importance to the State, viewed in the aggregate, that a victory should cost it, say, ·0001 of its adult population or ·00005—there is always superfluous labour enough to make good the difference—but it is vital to its very existence that the War should only last three months instead of three years. Hence it pays economically to be lavish with the lives of one's men, not merely on the battlefield, where, in fact, the men arrange matters mostly for themselves, but on the march, in bivouacs, etc., in fact by exacting from them individual exertions which break down ten for each one which bullets claim.

In Frederick's day, and generally in purely agricultural States, the work of a few individuals more or less, mattered little; in an advanced industrial State it is not only the sum of individual work withdrawn from productive labour, but the absence of even one particular man, head of a firm, for instance, which may paralyse the productive energy of thou-

41

sands.[1] This is the weak point of modern conscription, and entails upon the Nation, as a whole, the necessity of straining every nerve to secure a rapid decision, notwithstanding that, as a consequence, half-trained men have to be sent into the field and thousands of needless casualties incurred as a consequence of their individual inefficiency.

It has already been pointed out that the problem of the Infantry attack was identical in the old Smoothbore days with that which confronts us still, viz. to induce men to get as close to their enemy as possible before passing out of their leader's control and opening fire on their own account.

In detail it was solved then as it is now—sometimes one formation met the emergency, sometimes another; but the old view of the matter was, that the leader by the nature of the case, could be the only judge of which particular formation would best suit the immediate need; hence implicit obedience was demanded to his 'order," and the responsibility for the "order "itself rested on the Commander.

Starting from this point of view, the drill-book contained only rules for the execution of certain manoeuvres, but gave no instructions as to the application of these movements in the field. All such advice was circulated in more or less secret instructions issued to the several ranks, and the troops grew into the spirit of them through practice in drills and manoeuvres.

In War this answered well enough, for a man selected for promotion for good conduct in face of the enemy had generally intelligence enough to appreciate his new point of view quickly. But in peace, where promotion went by seniority, the practice was fatal, for as men grew up to a certain routine, their brains became atrophied by disuse, and when placed in positions of responsibility they proved entirely incapable of grappling with their difficulties.

---

1. See *War and the World's Life,* by the Author.

A further weakness lay in the fact that up to the close of the Seven Years' War, Line troops had been kept for Line fighting only. All skirmishing and outpost duties had been performed by irregular troops called "Freischaaren," enlisted, for the duration of the War from all the most uncontrollable natures in the country; men who loved fighting for fighting's sake and the prospects of loot—by robbing the dead and dying too frequently—that War brought in its train. These men had unwritten Light Infantry traditions of their own, which disappeared on their disbandment, and though all troops picked up hints from their experience, and passed them on to the recruits round the guard-room fire—by no means the worst way of imparting information—these points were forgotten as the war-seasoned men passed away, and few of the younger men or officers after twenty years of peace had any practical knowledge of them at all.

This was by far the gravest source of weakness in the whole Prussian Army. It was not the direct and positive duty of any one rank to teach intellectually the ranks beneath them. Hence no one ever learnt anything thoroughly, for it is only by teaching others that the average mind ever finds out its own weak places.

The want of the old "Freischaaren," however, soon made itself felt even in peace time, and as the news of British experiences against the revolted colonists in North America filtered over to Prussia, through Hessians, Hanoverians, and soldiers of fortune generally, attempts were made to create the nucleus of a permanent substitute for them, and the plan adopted was practically identical with our own.

The "musketeer" battalions threw off "light" companies specially trained to Light Infantry service; these being armed with the lighter musket known all over Europe as the "Fusil" were called "Fusiliers," and their value being much appreciated, whenever a brigade was put together, the "Fusilier companies" were grouped under one commander, and presently became a "battalion," with its own distinctive drill and uniform. This is a universal phenomenon which has always repeated itself, and originates from the instinct in every unit to become self-supporting. Thus Grenadiers grew from the men picked for strength and gallantry who were needed to precede assaulting columns in the Netherlands. Battalion guns have grown into "Batteries"—and "Maxims" have taken their place in the battalion. Mounted Infantry have grown in the same way, and doubtless each fresh need will be met by the same natural and normal growth, in spite of the outcry invariably raised that such a procedure ruins the parent stem from which the growth originally springs.

The Fusilier battalions, having thus evolved into distinct units, the need for light troops was again felt by the musketeers, and met in Prussia in rather an extraordinary way.

The Prussians, like all other European races, had retained the three ranks for Line formations long after all need for the third one had disappeared, if, in fact, it had ever existed. Actually all experienced men in every Army had condemned it as both useless and even dangerous, for once the first volley had been fired, nothing would induce troops under fire to conform to the regulations, which laid down that the front rank after standing up to load, as of course it had to do, should drop on the knee before firing again. The men simply would not conform to the order, and as the muskets were not long enough for the three ranks to fire all three standing, the rear rank either stood idle in well-drilled troops, or fired wildly in the air to keep up their spirits, in badly trained units.

An attempt was made to stop this practice by ordering the rear rank to load for the middle rank, exchanging muskets at every shot, but again the order came into direct conflict with human nature, and lapsed into a dead letter—for nothing would induce a trained soldier to part with his trusted

44

weapon, and also nothing would induce any soldier to fire off a musket which he had not loaded himself—a feeling which any one who has ever fired off a double charge can easily understand.

To make some use of this otherwise useless rank, some local commanders hit on the idea of employing its members as skirmishers, and this was the origin of the celebrated "Schützen Zug" or "skirmishing division" of the Prussian Company column, with all the complicated drill which its retention for so long involved. The practice soon became general, and rifled carbines were issued in certain proportions to the picked men of the third rank who were specially trained at target practice.

Covered by this screen of light troops it was evident to the Line battalions that their Commander was in a position to consider his decisions, and hence had a right to exact their due execution. As long as the skirmishers were working in front of them, men might be falling all around them, but it was obvious that the time for their independent action had not arrived, and all they had to do for the moment was to assist their leader, by prompt obedience to his orders, to place them in the best possible position to use their fire-power to the fullest possible extent.

Hence there was a clearly apparent justification for the obedience and accuracy of movement exacted from them, and if, in fact, some of the movements practised in peace seemed of little practical use in War, these were retained because the experience of the leaders had taught them all that, with the material at their disposal, the constant practice of intricate movements was the best means of ensuring that simple ones would be executed under fire.

This was an empirical conclusion, in fact, but one which is nevertheless psychologically correct, for the ceaseless repetition of the same routine dulls the intellect of the men after a time, and renders them more liable to panic reaction when confusion sets in, than is the case when the men have been taught to keep alert, and always learning something, by the practice of complicated manoeuvres.

In fact, in War, nothing complicated ever was attempted, and the utmost demanded from the men was an accurate deployment and a steady advance in line or in echelon in quick time (108 paces to the minute) until fire had to be opened, when, except against half-beaten troops, no one ever expected the men to go forward again without the impulse of fresh reinforcements from behind. The final stage of every attack was then precisely what it is now, (and must always remain, whatever drill books may prescribe,) a wild surging rush forward, officers leading, men of different units intermingled, and nobody troubling at all about dressing the ranks.

In principle, the halt to fire was delayed as long as possible; in peace it generally began at 200 yards, at which distance about 50 per cent, of the bullets might be counted on to take effect on a six foot target, but in War, the 200 yards often became 600 and even 800, according to the relative quality of the opposing troops, so that as a rule a special order was issued to the effect that those Commanders of regiments would most recommend themselves to the King who marched boldly on the enemy with "shouldered arms." It was never intended or expected that it either would or could be literally obeyed, but it was meant to strengthen the authority of the leader over his men, and to justify his insistence on the very utmost they could stand before opening fire.

When that fire of the Prussian Infantry began it was truly an appalling thing, as the casualty lists of their enemies show—for thanks to their ceaseless drilling, even as late as 1806, the Prussians went into action with a superiority over the French, in their rate of fire, quite as marked as that which the breechloader secured for them over the Austrians in 1866; and it was no fault of the men in the ranks that this advantage was not employed to greater profit.

As above pointed out, the essence of the old "Line" attack lay in the weight of metal thrown per unit of time, which again depended on the skill of the men and the utilization of every musket in the firing line. If all went well then the fire of the line swept away the enemy like a veritable scythe of death, and in proportion as this ideal was attained, the need of reserves was reduced to the minimum, and indeed, as many of our battles in India proved,[1] no reserves of Infantry at all were necessary. Hence there were no following lines to act as stop-butts for the enemy's "overs," and no lives were uselessly wasted, as is the case where heavy masses of men have to be kept at hand under a fire, they can do nothing to diminish, waiting for contingencies which may never arise. This forms the justification for the statement, that the old "Line "tactics constituted, in fact, the most economic investment of their soldiers' lives that Commanders could possibly make.

The point will become clearer as we deal with the French Army in the following chapter.

---

1. It is unnecessary to dwell on the exploits of the British Line in the Peninsula—where, in fact, two Lines generally sufficed—but it is often forgotten that in India, against enemies as well armed and quite as well drilled as any French troops we ever encountered; Lord Lake, who learnt his earliest lessons in the Seven Years' War, was at this very time demonstrating the fundamental strength of this idea. Thus at the battle of Delhi he attacked in a single deployed line of battalions, his only reserve being in Cavalry, which had already charged home three times that day—see also Laswari—and in later days, Sir Charles Napier at Miani and Hyderabad, to mention only the first examples that occur to me.

CHAPTER 2

The French Army Before Jena

As we have seen in the previous chapter, the era of military reform in France dates from the Battle of Roszbach, where, owing to their general slowness and want of manoeuvring power, the French Army was surprised on the march and ridden over with a catastrophic violence which has no parallel in history. Four-fifths of their previous experience having been gathered in the protracted wars in the Netherlands and on the Upper Rhine in the attack of fortresses and field entrenchments, the idea of the "assaulting column," not "fire power" lay at the root of their tactical reasoning. The connexion is well worth establishing, for in both cases there is always ample time for the columns to get into position, and though the success of the assault is of course only the consequence of a fire superiority previously acquired, this acquisition was always an entirely separate operation due to the combined action of Artillery and Engineers, with which the Infantry had no concern. But their intrusion into the rolling plains of Northern Germany brought them face to face with entirely novel conditions, and the working brains of the Army—the officers drawn from the "petit noblesse," the backbone and soul of the whole organization, were quick to see that mobility and precision were the whole essence of their future existence.

There followed, as usual, a thirty year struggle, the lifetime of a whole military generation, to carry these new ideas into execution, and only in 1791 was a regulation finally approved, so supple and sufficient that it lasted, almost without appreciable alteration, all through the Wars of the Revolution and Napoleon's time until 1822; indeed, much of its spirit remains in the Infantry Manual of the present day.[1]

It is the custom to picture the old Royal Army of France as an effete monarchical institution which did not survive the birth throes of the new dispensation, but, in fact, nothing could well be more diametrically opposed to the truth; it was the conservative spirit innate in all sound military institutions that absorbed the successive concussions of the social cataclysm, and though shaken and modified in the process, the Army nevertheless emerged with sufficient vitality and cohesion to form the fulcrum for all subsequent and enduring reforms. For generations the Army had been the sole career open to the younger sons of the nobility, men whose relative poverty kept them away from the corrupting atmosphere of a decidedly dissolute court, and compelled them to throw themselves heart and soul into their work, for there was nothing else to occupy their minds. This kind of service always brings its own reward, in the abiding love and affection of one's men; and when the storm came the great majority of the French Regiments stood firm against all temptations, and carried out their duties of repression and conciliation with a tact and temper beyond all praise.

There were exceptions, of course, but the fact remains that when Royalty was finally abolished, and by law, all commissions lapsed, the men almost invariably re-elected their

---

1. The dates of the several provisional regulations for Infantry issued by the French War Office were: 1750, '53, '54, '55, '64, '66, '69, '74, '75, '76,—1788, 1791—of these the draft of 64, drawn up by Marshal de Broglie, has been the model for all its successors. Colin, p. xii.

officers, and supported them against all the accusations and intrigues of the "representatives of the people."

It was on these men that the task devolved of breaking into shape the countless recruits, and drilling the swarms of volunteers, attracted to the colours by the pressure of starvation; and how well they did their work is shown by the fact that already at Jemappes in 1792—i.e., when the average service could hardly have exceeded six months—so numerous had been the desertions at first—these volunteer battalions, officered by civilians, only drilled by regulars, advanced in line of columns to within 400 yards of the muzzles of forty guns, and then deployed into line "as steadily as in peace time."[1]

But though they "deployed as steadily" they did not in fact continue their advance in line with the same steadiness, but "broke back" under a punishment, in face of which the twenty years' service men of their opponents would have hardly winced. Hence a double reason for the line of small handy columns—in general, battalion columns of about 500 men—arose. A broken attack breaking back on the front of a deployed line would have carried the latter away in their flight—hence wide intervals had to be kept to allow the debris of defeat to get out of the way, and when that debris had cleared the front, the enemy in pursuit was close upon the heads of the columns who now found it too late to deploy; and as they had to go on, the columns attacked as they stood, with the bayonet, because they could do nothing else.

It must also be remembered that unlike the Prussians during the Seven Years' War, the French were at first markedly inferior in the Cavalry Arm, and hence were compelled to move in formations which could readily adapt themselves to the needs of a Cavalry charge.

From our own experience since 1870, it is easy to judge that the reformers of the drill-books met with a most determined

---

1. *La Bataille de Jemappes, La Jonquiere,* p. 168.

resistance from the old school, all the more obstinate, indeed, because these men took their business more seriously than was the custom in our own service forty years ago. Civilians also took part in the struggle, and countless pamphlets were issued criticising each fresh tentative regulation or amendment, quite in the modern style. These latter being widely circulated, passed over into foreign countries, and the councils of the authorities remaining confidential, an entirely false view of French tactical thought was formed, which appeared to derive confirmation from what their adversaries actually saw of French methods during the first few years of the Revolutionary Wars.

With the light recent publications have shed on the subject, it is easy to see how the widespread misunderstandings underlying contemporary tactical criticism arose.

We now know that the French Generals endeavoured to fight their early battles almost entirely on the Prussian lines. They covered their front with light troops, (the "voltigeurs,") exactly as Frederick the Great had covered his advance with his "Freischaaren," and as we always did with our own "light" companies. But the manoeuvring power of their short service troops being much below that of their long service opponents, and the ground generally being more broken, they worked in lines of small columns to a greater extent, and often postponed deployment until it was absolutely forced upon them by the enemy's round shot, when it was very rarely made with the same precision as on a peace parade, though on occasion, no doubt, this may have occurred. Seen from the front, these compulsory deployments, or even the advances of half-drilled troops in line, must have appeared very ragged indeed to men accustomed to the punctilious and stately advance of their own much steadier troops,[1] and the observers,

---

1. A curious illustration of this opinion is afforded by a recent account of the French view of the attack of the XI Prussian Corps from Gunstett across the meadows towards the Niederwald in the Battle of Woerth (August 6, 1870), which is given in Kunz, p. 62. Part 13.

with their minds already full of the theories of the French pamphleteers advocating the advance *"en debandade"* and the advantages of the *"ordre profonde"* or columns as better suited to the irresistible *elan* of their countrymen, naturally jumped to the conclusion that these ragged attacks were intentional, not forced upon them by pressure of circumstances, and that the secret of French victories was to be found in the new form which the Revolution, with its hatred of order and control, had devised.

The real truth, however, is that the French deplored this absence of steadiness as much as we or the Prussians would have done in their place, and whilst the junior ranks and "progressives "of all Armies were ceaselessly bombarding their War Offices with proposal for upsetting the old and tried system of the Frederickan Line, the French were straining every nerve to get their men steady enough to preserve order under fire, and in the meanwhile, since they had to fight as best they could, their officers were learning to grapple with their difficulties and evolving a system which enabled them to fight to the best advantage, no matter in what ground they might happen to find themselves.

They did not abandon the attack by whole Divisions in Line or echelon, because such movements were vicious in principle, (which of course they never were, or can be,) but because in the first place their Leaders lacked the requisite experience to lead such "Lines "when the opportunity occurred; and in the second place, because the policy which dictated their strategy and in turn its methods, rarely threw them into country in which such attacks would have been practical, and where, in fact, we or the Prussians, would equally have been compelled to modify our own procedure, as, indeed, we often did in the spurs and mountainous country of the Peninsula.

Generally, by the time Napoleon began his career, the French Infantry had learnt to rely upon itself anywhere, to fight as skirmishers when they had to, or in Line where and whenever they could, and to manoeuvre with celerity in every situation, whereas the junior officers in the ranks of their opponents, who had never seen fighting of the intensity of that of the Seven Years' War, failed to understand the necessity for the severe training their more experienced seniors imposed upon them. Thus in 1791 they lost confidence in their own methods, and when defeat came upon them, were only too ready to throw the blame on the system which they did not understand, rather than on the failure of the strategic methods imposed upon them by their adherence to a system of recruiting which social changes was rapidly malting obsolete.

True Line tactics in those days, when it took two years to fit a soldier for the performance of his duties in the ranks, were only possible for long service Armies of specialists.[1] As soon as circumstances compelled nations to fight with short service levies a more elastic system had to be improvised, not that such systems were theoretically better, but because they alone were practicable.

At the outbreak of the Revolution the Army numbered 79 French and 23 Foreign Infantry Regiments; 12 battalions of Chasseurs, 7 Artillery Regiments, 26 Regiments of Heavy Cavalry, 18 Dragoons, 6 of Hussars, and 12 of Chasseurs à Cheval (Mounted Light Infantry), totalling in all 175,000 men. Behind them stood a militia of 55,000 to 70,000 men, and, as a kind of reservoir upon which to draw, 2,571,700 "National Guards," without any organization or even arms, who in obedience to a proclamation had enrolled themselves voluntarily, to escape the danger of being forcibly pressed for the front. Here and there a few battalions had organized themselves to protect their own property from the violence

---

1. Compare above, p. 26, chap. I. The new system ended by concentrating 70,000 men to the mile of front, that is to say, that though not more than 5,000 men could find useful employment for their muskets on that front, 65,000 men cumbered the ground behind as stop butts for the enemy's "overs."

of the mob, and these organizations, according to Thièbault, became fairly efficient units, and formed useful schools of arms, from which later many good officers were derived.

A proposal to introduce a stringent law of compulsory service had been rejected by a large majority of the Chambers, as out of harmony with the principles for which the Revolution was contending; hence, when in 1791 the War clouds burst over it, the Government of the moment had to help itself by a series of expedients from day to day.

Though, as pointed out above, the Regiments as a whole stood firm in their allegiance to the country, each Regiment had to undergo a little revolution within itself to adapt itself to its new situation, and, needless to say, these readjustments were not carried out without much suffering and many instances of personal hardships; yet about two-thirds of the whole seem to have held together and formed a sufficiently strong nucleus to digest their new recruits.

These, however, were at first difficult to find, for instead of expanding existing "cadres "in a normal manner, the Assembly decreed in July, 1791, the formation of 169 Volunteer battalions, recruited from the enrolled National Guards. This decree was received with enthusiasm in Paris, and in a few days no less than three battalions were formed, but there the enthusiasm began to flicker out, and by September 25 only sixty were available for service, and very few of these appear to have reached the front. These men, however, were only called upon to serve for the "Campaign "which, according to the custom of the period was held to terminate, quite irrespective of the enemy's ideas, on December 1, and as they also received whilst enrolled a higher rate of pay than the line, the latter found themselves deprived of their supply of recruits and dwindled away visibly.

The confusion and want of discipline in this first levy were quite appalling. The Generals at the front were loud in their denunciation of these armed bandits, who robbed the inhabitants of their own country, and set the worst kind of examples to the Regular troops, and they clamoured for their withdrawal and replacement by troops of the Line. But the Committee of Public Safety saw in their unanimity, a subtle design against the Revolution, and instead of stemming the evil, aggravated it by decreeing the formation of a further 45 battalions, additional to the original 169, only 60 of which were in actual existence (May 5, 1792), all of the 214 to be brought up to a strength of 800 men.

On June 1,1792, the Regular Army numbered 178,000 men, of whom 90,000 stood in face of the enemy. Of the Volunteers there appear to have been altogether 84,000 under arms, but these were the best, who had resisted the temptations to desert, or having tried the remedy, had found it worse than the disease and returned to the colours, resigned to make the best of things. But these numbers were entirely inadequate to confront the gathering hosts of the Coalition, and on July 11 the celebrated declaration, *"La patrie en danger,"* was issued, which called upon all men of an age to bear arms to consider themselves "mobilized," and to chose from their own districts those men who were to march first against the enemy.

These men were no longer to be known as "Volunteers "but were designated *"Federes,"* because the battalions in which they were to march had no longer any territorial connexion, but were put together from several departments, and were destined to recruit the Line, the Volunteers already at the front, and complete those units most advanced in formation, etc. A number of "Free Companies" of Chasseurs were also to be formed. The result, however, was disappointing. Up to September 20 this proclamation brought in only 60,000 men, of whom not half reached the front, barely sufficient to make good the ordinary wastage. Yet it was with troops formed under such dispiriting conditions that Dumouriez won the Battle of Jemappes—and the reason is not far to seek—only the best had survived their ordeals and reached the front.

In face of this state of affairs, and the addition of Great Britain to the ranks of their enemies, the National Convention was compelled to abandon the idea of Voluntary service, and on February 20, 1793, it decreed a compulsory levy of 300,000 men, distributed over the several communes, each of which was to issue an appeal for men to make up its quota, and if in three days the number was incomplete, the balance was to be made good by recourse to the ballot urn.

All unmarried National Guards between the ages of eighteen and forty were held liable for service.

At the same time, to put an end to the friction which had existed between the soldiers of the Regular Army and the Volunteers, the old white coat was taken away from the former, all alike were compelled to wear the dark blue of the National Guard, and a new unit was instituted, the "demi brigade," which consisted of a regular battalion, and one or two Volunteer battalions, both retaining their own special peculiarities, other than the colour of their coats.

Yet the French Army survived even this extraordinary measure, and it was with troops brigaded together in this wise that Napoleon won his victories in Italy in 1796—for the order by which the final "amalgam," as it was called, of Line and Volunteers, by which the latter were finally absorbed into the line, only reached the Army of Italy a few days before he assumed the command, and was put into execution during the course of the campaign.

This, however, in anticipation, and in the meanwhile French recruiting had many vicissitudes to endure. The proclamation was meeting with little success, when the news of Dumouriez's defeat at Neerwinden (March 18, 1793), was received, and a perfect panic of terror seized the Nation. The "Committee of Public Safety "was elected, and forthwith proceeded to most drastic steps. Decree after decree was issued, each wilder than the other, until, on

March 23, Barère's suggestions became law[1] and hundreds of thousands of men were driven to arms and despatched towards the frontier.

The internal paralysation of France was now complete, for these men robbed and plundered wherever they appeared, and deserted by tens of thousands. In a few months the desolation of the country was so complete that absolutely no other refuge for a man remained, where he could be reasonably secure against denunciation and hunger, except at the front. Then the tide turned and the Army began to receive a healthier and better type of recruit, men who having had their fill of freedom, recognized at last the value of discipline and order, and henceforward submitted with reasonable willingness to necessary restraint.

As the period of extreme terror and tension relaxed, the

---

1. The preamble of the celebrated decree of August 23, 1793, drawn up by Barere, is as follows—"Jusqu'au moment ou les ennemis auront été chasses du territoire de la Republique, tous les Francais sont en requisition permanente pour le service des armees—Les jeunes gens iront au combat; les hommes maries forgeront les armes et transporteront les subsistances; les femmes feront des tentes, des habits, et serviront dans les hopitauz; les enfants mettront le vieux linge en charpie; *les vieillards se feront porter sur les places publiques* pour exciter le courage dee guerriers, la haine des rois et le devouement de la Republique Les maisons rationales seront convertis en casernes; la sol des caves sera lessive pour en extraire le salpetre, etc., etc., and articles 8, 9, laid down, Nul ne pourra se *faire remplacer* dans le service pour lequel il sera requis; les fonctionaires publics reste—ront a leur postes—*La Levle sera generate,* les citoyens non maries ou veufs sans enfants de 18 a 25 marcherent les premiere," but nothing is said as to when they return. Assuming, however, that the population of France at that date was in round numbers 30,000,000, then the annual contingent would be 300,000 men, of whom 200,000 would be physically fit to bear arms. If the duration of service be taken as from 18 to 60 years of age, then, in a population whose average death rate would be, say, 40 per thousand, the normal death rate of healthy males between these ages would not exceed 15 per thousand. That is to say, there should have been in France about 6 million men available to answer this appeal. Actually it appears that on January 1, 1794, not more than 770,000 were present under arms, and there was one official at home for every two soldiers at the front. The estimates for 1793, which were, in fact, largely exceeded, make the average cost of these soldiers 1,800 francs, an enormous figure for those days, principally accounted for by cost of new arms and equipment and leakage.

defects in the drafting of this decree of 1793 became more and more evident, and the whole subject of Army Reform occupied again and again the attention of the succeeding Governments, until finally the whole was recast and submitted to the Council of Five Hundred by General Jourdan, and it was finally decreed (September 5, 1798) that every Frenchman was liable to military service from his twentieth to twenty-fifth year, and to the men thus liable the term *"defenseurs consents "is* applied for the first time.

How many of these men were to be called out and for how long depended on circumstances—whether the country was at War or not. There was no fixed term of service qualifying for dismissal to the Reserves; apparently no intention of forming any, and since for the next seventeen years the country was never at peace for more than three consecutive years, it would seem that the term of service was practically fixed by the man's ability to bear arms, and by nothing else. As the actual deaths during these years actually exceeded one million, though by how many it is impossible to state, it is evident that even a moderate rate of invaliding would have barely kept pace with the supply. It will be seen that this law permitted no exemption except from physical causes, and its operation pressed so intolerably upon the people in their shattered condition, that in the following year (1800) the provision of a paid substitute was sanctioned, and continued in force until 1870, when it proved one of the principal causes of the French downfall, as in practice it allowed the bulk of the middle classes to escape service, thus throwing the burden of defence on the upper and lower, "the froth and the dregs," to use an expression often applied to it by the opponents of the system. In the space at my disposal it is utterly impossible to convey any adequate picture of the Administrative work which fell upon the French War Office during this period in which Minister after Minister succeeded one another in rapid succession, and only Carnot, a Captain of Engineers, remained permanent.

I have alluded above to the creation of the "demi brigades "and the "amalgams "in which Regulars, and Volunteers were brigaded side by side, and ultimately fused altogether. Each of these steps entailed the disruption of hundreds of Volunteer units, and the absorption of thousands of officers, who, it is hardly necessary to add, resented their supersession or removal, almost in proportion to their original unfitness for their posts. But the step gave the authorities the much-needed power of selection, which they seem to have exercised with considerable discretion, judging from the uniform excellence of the commanders whom Napoleon took over when he became Emperor. Theirs was, indeed, a case of the "survival of the fittest "in a terribly hard school of selection, for not only had they been compelled to justify themselves by their acts in the face of the enemy, but to maintain control over their men, in spite of all risks of secret denunciation and political animosity.

Only born leaders of men could have survived such an ordeal. They may have been, indeed they often were, illiterate, rapacious, jealous and vindictive, but they all possessed that power which defies all examinations to elicit, *viz.*, the power to get the last ounce of exertion and self-sacrifice out of the men under them, without recourse to legal formalities, or the application of authorized force.

In a word, they were "crowd leaders," men who knew instinctively in each successive rank how to keep the dominant sentiment of the mass upon their side. When, for instance, at a later period Napoleon kept a whole Hussar brigade out under a heavy artillery fire as a punishment for unsteadiness in a previous action, he knew he was safe in doing so, because the majority of the Army strongly disapproved of cowardice under fire. But he would have been quite powerless to compel the same Hussars to groom their horses up to the Prussian standard, because the whole weight of opinion in the Service was against such a practice, and this tendency ran through every grade of the whole Army and in itself constituted a moral factor sufficient to account almost entirely for its numerous successes.

In long service Armies, trained in peace time, this "art of command "is generally absent, for nothing ever occurs to compel a young officer to exert the spark of it which in varying degrees we all possess. In a wise system of training things would be so arranged that such opportunities would have to be faced, but this is difficult, as they are always unpopular to all except the "elect," who rejoice in them. Still in our own case, with the facilities our Territorial system presents, it would be easy to arrange for such an interchange of officers from time to time amongst the several battalions, that all should find an opportunity of learning how to enforce obedience without recourse to authority, *and in that way we might find a compensation for many defects in our organization when it is compared with the machine-like exactitude of other nations.*

It was out of these difficult circumstances by which the French officers were surrounded that the system of decentralization of command which led to the formation, first, of the "Division," ultimately to that of the "Army Corps "developed.

Since without ingrained respect for the "rank" mutual personal knowledge between men and officers was the only bond which could be relied upon, it became the custom to keep the General who had won the confidence of his men at the head of the same units as long as possible, and then to give him the freest possible hand in their command. It had, of course, long been the practice to place Generals at the heads of detachments of the three Arms, which were, in fact, Corps, but these detachments were only formed *ad hoc,* and generally melted away into the Army when they rejoined Headquarters. There was no distinct bond of connexion between the units and their Commander, and above all, no staff mechanism for the circulation of orders to units. During the early years of the Revolutionary Wars, when an

Austrian General wished to order an operation, he had to write, or cause to be written by his clerks, separate orders in detail to each of the units in his command, a process in which so much time was lost that the orders almost invariably arrived too late.[1] The French Corps Commander had merely to send an order to each of his three or four units, who then passed on the essential portion of each to the Brigades, and so forth, according to the system of the present day, and in this lay the chief secret of their superior mobility. There is nothing to show that a Prussian or Austrian battalion could not march as fast and as far along a high road as a French one—indeed, the presumption is that both in physique and in training the latter were inferior to the longer service men of other nations; but the fact remains that, whereas French Army Corps could average twenty miles a day and could be pushed to thirty-five, their enemies, owing to this vicious want of system in the circulation of orders, could rarely manage ten miles a day, and often fell as low as six and seven.

This was the essential secret of French mobility on which in turn Napoleon's strategy depended, and in no campaign is its advantage more apparent than in the one under consideration, *for had the French averaged five miles a day less, the whole combination of Jena would have been impossible.*

Lastly, we must call attention to an innovation in the conduct of War, due to Carnot's genius, which though in advance of the means at his disposal, formed the stepping-stone for Napoleon's progress. We have seen that it had been the custom to form detachments of all arms for special missions in all countries, but it had never occurred to any one to use these detachments in combination for a special offensive. When, for instance, Frederick the Great

---

1. See two complaints, one by Beaulieu in 1796, the other by Mack in 1805, both clamouring for more clerks in the Austrian K.A.

projected an offensive, he united his whole Army for the purpose, only leaving behind such detachments as were necessary for purely defensive purposes—they might within their own sphere operate offensively—for the attack was generally admitted as the soundest form of defence—but their movement was never combined with the main Army on an ulterior objective.

Carnot initiated the idea of combining the operations of several Armies, two or more, in an advance on a single objective, such as Vienna in 1796, in which the Armies of Jourdan from the lower Rhine, of Moreau from the middle Rhine, and of Napoleon in Italy were all directed upon Vienna. As already stated, the idea was beyond the means of execution available—wireless telegraphy alone would have justified the risk—but it formed the point of departure for Napoleon's principle of combining his Army Corps upon the battlefield to which all his subsequent successes were due.

It is now time to turn to the specific development of the latter's methods and to trace step by step how these evolved themselves into a definite system, the essence of which was, that no matter what the enemy did, or did not do, Napoleon was certain to unite a numerical superiority against him.

In his *Education Militaire de Napoleon,* Capt. Colin of the French General Staff has traced for us the gradual evolution of Napoleon's executive talent up to the Campaign of 1796, showing us the books he read and the type of mind with which he was brought into contact. Col. Camon of the French Engineers has given us an admirable study of the spirit of the Emperor's Campaigns as derived from his own orders and correspondence; and we have in addition the admirable investigations of General Bonnal and General Foch, all from the standpoint of modern criticism, and based on the material found in the Archives of the French War Ministry.

These studies throw an entirely new light on the working

of Napoleon's mind from day to day, and more especially enable us to discount the "evidential" value of his own Memoirs written at St. Helena, also those of his Marshals and other contemporaries.

We no longer see him making plans of campaign complete to the smallest detail, far in advance of events, for we are now able to follow him from day to day, with a great objective undeniably before him, but working for it by fresh resolutions conceived from hour to hour, as the reports of the enemy's movements came to hand; and meeting each emergency as it arose with an intuitive perception which at times seems little short of miraculous.

In his first Italian Campaigns we find him still practising the precepts of his masters, which were indeed time-honoured and accepted by all his contemporaries in theory; but whereas they were tied and bound by practical considerations of supply and responsibility, he was relatively free from these restrictions. Hence he was able to apply them with a vigour and boldness to which the eighteenth century could afford no parallel. Concentration on the decisive point was no novelty; every other General of the period would gladly have anticipated his example had they been able to do so, but because of the utter want of system for circulating information and orders which prevailed in their armies, Napoleon's concentration was always finished first.

Nor was there a General in Europe who was not equally well aware of the advantage to be gained by threatening an enemy's communications; most of them knew only too well from bitter experience how fatally demoralizing to the troops was the mere rumour of danger to their lines of supply and retreat; but they knew, as practical men, that the threat at their enemy's communication involved the exposure of their own, and that as opposed to Napoleon they had the most to lose.

For the French had been forced by circumstanced to learn to do without luxuries, and dragged no interminable train behind them. If the enemy captured their bivouac grounds, they were no better off than before, for the Republican troops left no supplies behind them, whereas if their enemy succeeded in manoeuvring them out of their positions, it was in practice impossible to prevent their finding food, arms, equipment and ammunition. If they failed in their undertakings, they had an outraged King and Cabinet to face and an established position to lose. If Napoleon failed he risked only his head, and heads sat lightly on French shoulders during those first terrible years.

The conditions, therefore, were quite unequal, and it needed only audacity and the driving energy of an almost superhuman character to carry the French Army to victory. It was this need that Napoleon abundantly supplied, but it was a very risky game to play; and when at Marengo his concentration failed, *for the reason that he had allowed his enemy time to concentrate first,* he set his mind to work to find some safer basis for his projects, and found it for the moment *in the training of his Cavalry to form the "Cavalry Screen."*

It was in reliance on this system that he entered upon the Campaign of Ulm in 1805. Covered by a Cavalry screen a couple of days' march in front of his Infantry columns, he adapted his manoeuvres to the movements of his enemy quite in the manner of the modern German school, whose practice in 1870 shows no advance upon his original conception. But Napoleon soon found out *that though Cavalry could observe, it possessed in itself no power to hold;* and it was quickly evident to him *that the presence of an enemy at a given spot on a given date was no sure indication of where that enemy might happen to be forty-eight hours later.*

The problem is, in fact, insoluble, for only the other side can be aware of all the factors which enter into the decision, and even then no two minds are likely to appreciate these several factors at the same valuation.

The practical solution he ultimately discovered and applied is indicated by his well-known maxim, *"On ne ma-noeuvre pas qu'autour d'un point fixe "*; and his first employment of this principle will form the subject matter of the following pages.

In forming the "Grand Army" at Boulogne and in Holland during the years 1803-4-5, Napoleon only stereotyped the practice of his predecessors. The amount of time devoted to tactical or manoeuvring training was infinitesimal judged by the present standard, but the men and officers learnt to know one another and many incompetent persons were weeded out. It was this bond of comradeship and the knowledge of the daily incidents of war taught by the veterans to the young soldiers which constituted the real strength of the Army—for in organization as we now know it, it was in a very rudimentary state indeed. Owing to its having been formed primarily for the invasion of England, it possessed practically no commissariat trains at all and both the Artillery and Cavalry were very short of horses, and when the orders to march for the Danube were issued, many of the Dragoons started for the front on foot. Fortunately for the French the Austrians were in even worse case. They had taken the horses from their trains to strengthen their artillery and their Infantry, quite un-accustomed to fend for themselves, practically starved in the midst of plenty. The French did not.[1]

---

1. See Colin and Alombert, *La Grand Armés,* 1805, and *The Evolution of Modern Strategy,* by the author, which gives a short precis of the above monumental work.

CHAPTER 3

Prussian Movements to October 13th

The proximate cause of the Campaign of Jena was the violation of Hohenzollern territory by Napoleon's Army on the march to Ulm in September 1805. Bernadotte, acting under the Emperor's orders, had suddenly appeared before the gates of the little town of Ansbach, an outlying portion of the King of Prussia's dominions, at the head of an over-whelming mass of troops, and demanded free passage for his columns, on pain of hostilities if his request were refused. The weak little garrison, having no orders, had no choice, according to the code of the day, but to grant this demand to avert the effusion of blood.

This outrage against the Law of Nations was so flagrant that the King of Prussia immediately ordered the mobiliza-tion of his Army, then waited to see what would happen. His surprise, and that of his councillors, was immense, when, in fact, nothing whatever occurred, only the French columns pursued their way towards Ulm and ultimately to Vienna, without taking the least notice of the tentative threat. To un-derstand the situation it must be remembered that under Fre-derick the Great, Prussian mobilization had been worked out to the last detail, even as at the present day, and the threat to set this machinery in motion had for years been considered as the trump card of diplomacy, for until the creation of the Grand Army at Boulogne, no other power could approach the celerity with which Prussia could bring her forces to a War footing. The King's councillors were so convinced that in face of the threat which this mobilization conveyed, the French must immediately "climb down," that they had omitted altogether to determine what steps they should take in the circumstances which actually ensued, consequently they were not in the least prepared to take advantage of the magnificent opportunity Fortune now presented to them, by adding themselves to the ranks of Napoleon's enemies, and boldly falling across the communications of his Army with the Rhine. They temporized and negotiated, and meanwhile Napoleon steadily marched.

Austria had not precipitated the rupture with France without having arranged for the support of the Russians, and in order to draw Prussia into the coalition, the Emperor of Russia himself journeyed to Berlin, where supported by the influence of Queen Louise, of never-to-be-forgotten memory, he succeeded in persuading the King to throw his sword into the scale, should Napoleon prove deaf to a final appeal to make peace on the basis of the last European settlement at Pressburg.

This promise of alliance was solemnly sworn by the two Monarchs over the grave of Frederick the Great in Potsdam on the night of November 2-3 (1805), and an ultimatum to this effect was at once prepared by the Prussian Government.

The task of conveying this ultimatum to Napoleon was entrusted to Graf Haugwitz, a typical diplomatist of the old school, who bore exactly the same relation to the men of the school of Bismarck as a venerable county family solicitor bears to the modern railroad magnate of America. From his point of view, his young Master had been led into a most regrettable scrape by his wife and her friends, and it was for him to save as much of the estate as possible by making advantageous terms with the adversary. Haugwitz knew the might of the French military machine more thoroughly perhaps than any other Prussian of his day, and feeling perfectly certain that Napoleon must win the coming battle in Moravia, he determined to procrastinate until after the event, and then see if he could not pick up some pieces for his client out of the general destruction of Treaties and frontiers, which he shrewdly foresaw as the consequences of a French victory.

He delayed his departure from Berlin till November 14, and then journeyed so slowly, making the excuse of illness, that he only reached Brunn on November 28, but still some days too early to suit his purpose. He certainly had an interview with Napoleon on that day (see Corres. xi, 9560), but as neither of the two wished to discuss the situation until the decision of Arms had been given, no serious business appears to have been touched upon, and not until after the victory of Austerlitz did the diplomatist obtain an opportunity of delivering himself of his task. Needless to say, the form in which he presented his request was very different from the ultimatum he had been dispatched to convey, and after a few interviews with Talleyrand and the Emperor, he subscribed on behalf of his Sovereign the most pitiful treaty, from the point of view of national honour, to which the sanction of a reigning Monarch at the head of an unbeaten Army, burning with the desire to wipe out a national disgrace, has ever been appended.

By this Treaty, dated December 15, 1805, Prussia guaranteed to France in advance the terms she meant to exact from Austria and Russia; she ceded to France the principalities of Ansbach, Cleve, Neufchatel and Wesel, and in exchange took over from France, as by right of conquest, the Kingdom of Hanover, the property of the King of England.

Haugwitz himself seems to have been rather doubtful as to the reception this Treaty was likely to obtain in Berlin, for instead of despatching it by special courier, according to custom in such cases, he decided to be the messenger himself, and leaving Vienna on December 17, he reached Berlin on Christmas Day. Never was a Nation less grateful for a Christmas present. The Queen and the Army were furious, and for a moment it seemed possible that the whole proceeding would be repudiated. But the old diplomatists were still too strong, and the clause concerning Hanover having been modified so as to conceal "the act of Treachery"[1] meditated against England by the excuse of taking over the Kingdom "in Trust" for the final settlement on the conclusion of a General Peace, the Treaty was finally ratified, and Haugwitz was sent to Paris to obtain the Emperor's approval to the modification.

This, however, he very decidedly refused to give, and demanded not only that Hanover should be immediately occupied, but that Prussia should also close her ports against England, with the result that on June 11 England formally declared War against Prussia, and her ally, Sweden—a small detachment of whose troops had held portions of Hanoverian Territory in King George's interest—immediately followed suit.

Meanwhile, however, Prussia had demobilised her Army, but hardly had the troops settled down in their normal garrisons, when the French demands became more exacting, and Prussia was at length compelled to protest.

It is the conventional idea that from the first Napoleon deliberately planned to drive the latter into War, but the evidence hardly seems to bear out this conclusion, for his hands were sufficiently full with many internal affairs, and for the moment he had nothing to gain by hostilities. It seems more probable that he merely miscalculated the limits of Prussian endurance, for the fact remains that having withdrawn his troops from Austria and distributed them in wide can-

---

1. This is Clausewitz's expression. See *Naohrichten Über Preussen in seiner Groszen Katastrophe,* published by the Prussian General Staff in *Kriegtgeschichtlichen Einzdkeite,* No. 10, Berlin, 1888.

tonments all over the South of Germany, where they lived practically at free quarters, he left them there in complete repose, for riot one single order emanated to them from the War Office in Paris from the 14th February till September 1, 1806.[1] Nothing could illustrate more emphatically the extent to which decentralization of command had been carried in the French Army. Yet Prussia actually began to mobilize in the first week of August, and had approached both Saxony and Hesse-Cassel with a view to obtaining alliances, facts which did not escape the ubiquitous eyes of the French Secret Service.

It would indeed appear that the latter had been too well informed from its own standpoint. The public opinion of the Prussian masses, as opposed to the Prussian Court and Army, was by no means in the blaze of indignation which the fate of its very near neighbours might have been expected to evoke, for they were still completely under the illusion that War was merely a struggle between Governments, carried out with all possible respect for private interests, and it seemed to them a matter of indifference whether a few more hundred thousand fellow countrymen passed under the French yoke or remained under that of their own Monarch. There is no doubt that Napoleon and his agents, who still believed that they were bestowing freedom upon downtrodden nationalities, felt equally convinced that a few thousand inhabitants more or less would hardly be worth going to war about. But they had entirely overlooked the business point of view from which the old diplomatists would regard the matter, when the French, not content with what the Treaty already gave them, actually seized other districts to round off their estates, and proceeded to group all their acquisitions into a new Confederation, which would

---

1. Bonnal, *La Manoeuvre de Jena,* p. 2. There is one letter of July 11, but of no particular importance.

of necessity completely neutralize the confederation of the North-German States, which the Prussians themselves aspired to dominate.[1]

Notwithstanding the complete failure of their favourite trump card, mobilization, in the previous year, they were still so blind to the changed temper of the times, that they hazarded it again, as we have seen, during the first week in August. Apparently they were as confident of its efficacy as ever, for when the threat it conveyed fell perfectly flat, they found themselves quite without plans for the action that it was now incumbent on them to take.

Except with Saxony, who agreed to furnish a contingent of 20,000 men, they had completed no arrangements with their neighbours, who between them might have supplied another 80,000 men. They had made no arrangements for calling up reserves of men, money, or of arms, for placing the fortresses in a proper state of defence, or for creating bridgeheads over the principal rivers, or even for withdrawing existing stores from exposed districts, and but for the ready acquiescence in their change of policy by the courts of England, Russia and Sweden, they would have stood quite alone, with only 200,000 men to confront the onrush of Napoleon, who could and, if necessary, would have set in motion to

---

1. Clausewitz gives the following list of principal violations of the original treaty—**(a)** The creation of the Federation of the Rhine, immediately after the conclusion of the peace of Pressburg with Austria, although no word of any such design was included in that Treaty, and hence neither Austria or Prussia had received due warning of its inception. **(b)** Intrigues set on foot by France to hinder the formation of a North-German Confederation by Prussia, although France herself had suggested this Confederation as an equivalent for other sacrifices. **(c)** That France had offered to the Elector of Hesse the Bishopric of Fulda if he would join the Rhine Confederation, a district which belonged to the Prince of Orange, brother-in-law of the King of Prussia. **(d)** That the Grand Duke of Berg (Murat) had seized the Abbeys of Essen and Verden; although neither had belonged to the Duchy of Cleve (all that was ceded to him). **(e)** That France had appropriated the fortress of Wesel, although Prussia had only ceded it to the Grand Duke of Berg.

crush them, the whole of the resources of France, certainly not less than a million war-trained men.

The total military resources of the kingdom at this moment are given by Clausewitz as—

INFANTRY

58	Regiments of 2 battalions	99,760	
29	Grenadier battalions	19,952	
24	Fusilier battalions	16,512	
3	Rifles battalions	1,800	
5	Guards battalions	3,440	
	Total		**141,464**

CAVALRY

12	Cuirassier Regiments of 5 squadrons	7,920	
14	Dragoon Regiments—12 of 5 squadrons, 2 of 10 squadrons	10,560	
15	Squadrons of Lancers	2,430	
9½	Regiments of Hussars, of 10 squadrons each	15,390	
	Total, 250 squadrons		**36,300**

ARTILLERY

10	Horse Artillery batteries		
4	Regiments, Foot Artillery (not *field* Artillery)	8,000	
	Total strength of field troops		**185,764**

GARRISON & DEPOT TROOPS

58	Third battalions of 500 men	29,000	
58	Companies of Pensioners	2,900	
	Total Garrison and Depot troops		**31,900**
	GRAND TOTAL		**217,664**

Out of this number, as Clausewitz points out, 150,000 might have been made available for the field, but thanks to the idea then prevalent in the military world that since tactical reserves were desirable in battle, strategic reserves must be equally desirable in the Theatre of War, the whole of the Army was not mobilized simultaneously, and such large detachments were kept back in Poland and Silesia that actually the strength of the main Army in Thuringia never exceeded 110,000 men. Scharnhorst, indeed, puts it as low as 96,840 on the morning of the Battle of Jena.

Though both England and Russia had immediately abandoned any idea of hostilities against Prussia, the Cabinet were still so firmly convinced that the order for mobilization would suffice to cause the French to withdraw their pretensions, that they allowed their precious period of respite, during the months of August and September, to elapse without completing any definite treaties of alliance with either nation, but contented themselves with arranging the several commands for the Field Army, and appointing the necessary Staffs, and these were allotted more with a view to harmonize the claims and jealousies of their leaders than to facilitate their employment in the field.

These personalities now claim a share of our attention, as their respective idiosyncrasies did more, perhaps, to paralyse the potential fighting capacity of the Prussian Army than all other factors put together.

There were three men in the Prussian Forces whose claims to independent command it was impossible to ignore. First, Duke Carl of Brunswick, nephew and pupil of Frederick the Great, and reigning Sovereign of the Duchy from which he took his title. This Duchy actually claimed neutrality in the forthcoming struggle, a claim willingly conceded in the first instance by Prussia, but made short work of by the French when they approached its boundaries. The Duke's experience of War had hardly been fortunate, and though it had not seriously affected his reputation, it had certainly affected his nerve; but he had made himself indispensable at Court, and the idea of superseding him seems never to have been entertained. Presumably to strengthen his initiative, Scharnhorst was appointed to his Staff as Q.M.G., a measure by no means well received by the Army, for Scharnhorst was still only a Major and a Hanoverian. It was only too late that the Army discovered his real value, when in 1813 he died from wounds received at Bautzen.

Next came Prince Hohenlohe, now in his sixty-first year. His career in 1792-3 had been brilliant, and his personal courage was beyond dispute. He had also read much and had enjoyed the opportunity, rare in those days, of observing the French troops in the field and studying their methods,[1] but he lacked intellectual capacity to assimilate his information, and was easily led astray by a fluent conversationalist; and fate unkindly placed a very Prince of talkers at his elbow, in the person of Massenbach, subsequently known as the ".evil genius of Prussia," to whose career we shall presently return.

Last, stood the Prussian General, "von Rüchel," the concentrated essence of the Prussian Army," as Clausewitz calls him.[2] As a young officer he had been singled out by Frederick the Great, and had repaid that monarch by the most whole-souled devotion to his memory. "The King could do no wrong;" and though he had read, written, and seen much, everything had been referred back to this one standard, and appreciated not by its conformity with existing conditions, but with the acts and sayings of his master; who of course had a totally different set of facts to deal with.

He was a fluent and convincing speaker, but neither his speeches nor his writings, which were many, betray any real intellectual capacity. His principal claims to command rested on his abounding energy, absolute self-confidence, and power of inspiring the men immediately around him. As a drill-master he had no superior, and he possessed the utmost faith in what he taught. The organization of the troops into independent Divisions was only completed subsequent to their mobilization, and gave a total of fourteen commands, composed as shown in the accompanying order of battle, and more to mark the Royal appreciation of the three personalities referred to above, than in conformity with any strategical conception. These were assigned to them in the following proportions:

---

1. See v. d Goltz, *Roszbach und Jena,* 2nd Edition, p. 395. After the demobilization of 1805 he had visited his estates at Oehringen in Franconia, where the French then lay in cantonments. He had been provided with a guard of honour and lived on terms of intimacy with the French General Gudin and his Staff. 2. "Concentrated acid" is the exact word he uses, see *Nachrichten aus Preüssen,* p. 436. *G.st. K. E.,* p. 455.

The Principal Army, six Divisions; the Silesian Saxon Army, five Divisions; Rüchel's independent Corps, three Divisions. It was *à propos* of this arrangement that Clausewitz in his book *Vom Kriege* wrote that "there is no worse subdivision of an Army possible than one in three parts, excepting always one in two," and the justice of this criticism will frequently become apparent, for on the strength of the importance of the charge entrusted to them, Hohenlohe and Massenbach —-they must be henceforth thought of as *one, not two, individualities*—felt themselves justified in proposing their own plans of campaign, and endeavouring to compel the Duke of Brunswick to assist them in their execution.

Evidently this friction had been foreseen from the first, for to act as a brake on the independent initiative of both Commanders, the King had decided to accompany the Duke of Brunswick's Headquarters, taking with him the Army Council,[1] the Chief of the General Staff (Colonel Phull), and as his confidential adviser, the aged Field Marshal, von Mollendorf, who frankly admitted that he was no longer equal to the fatigues inseparable from an active command. All the Privy Councillors, diplomats, etc., of course went with the Court, even the Queen and her ladies felt they might be useful and would not be left behind.

A few words are necessary here to depict the characters of the principal actors in the subsequent events, otherwise no sufficient explanation of the fatal slowness which stamped the Prussian movements can ever be arrived at, or the responsibility for the final catastrophe be properly allocated, and the personality of the King himself is naturally the first to engage attention.

History has dealt far more harshly with the memory of this unfortunate Sovereign than the testimony of the actual facts will warrant. It was his misfortune to be called to the

---

1, The Ober Kriegs Kollegium created by Frederick William II, June 25, 1788, See Von der Golta.

governance of his country at a crisis of the first magnitude in its affairs, before age and experience might have enabled him to trust his own judgment and override the well-meant but pernicious advice that the council of greybeards, by whom he was surrounded, had freely tendered.

These men, who had shared in Frederick the Great's immortal triumphs, had risen by the exercise of those very talents whose possession is invariably fatal to the survival of genius. Each in his own department was an "expert" in the fullest sense of the term, admirable tools for the great Leader who knows how to employ "experts "and to compel each one to sacrifice his own interests for the good of the whole. To do this, however, needs more strength of character than is reasonably to be expected from a man of the King's years.

It is at all times a difficult task to emancipate oneself from the intellectual control of one's teachers, and it is immeasurably harder for a man without war-experience to override the mature conclusions of those who have lived in face of the enemy for years. It is only by degrees that one learns that in ninety-nine cases out of a hundred, *the value of War teaching ends with the man's rank at the time he underwent its lesson.*

That the King had in him the makings of the "Employer of Experts "his comments on the innumerable projects for reform preserved to us abundantly testify. He knew well enough that reform was necessary, but he knew also that there must be a *real driving spirit behind reforms to make them effective,* and of this spirit, and its corollary, *the willingness to make sacrifices in one's own department or person,* these several memoirs present not a trace.

Comparing him with that great reformer, Scharnhorst, and judging both by their subsequent actions, I submit, with all due deference to established authority, that at the fateful climax the King's mind was actually the riper of the two.

The Ober Kriegs Collegium, which I have translated freely by the title of Army Council, whom the King took with him to guide his councils, consisted of the several Inspector Generals and heads of departments, the Adjutant General and the Quarter-master General. It was therefore somewhat more cumbrous than our present institution, and hence was even less adapted for arriving at rapid decisions. The members in their individual capacity had all risen by punctilious attention to their office work, and the Quarter-master General in particular, Colonel Phull, had acquired notoriety by the invention of systems of strategy based on the topography of the Theatre of War, but not on the enemy's operations. It is principally against him that Clausewitz levelled his deadly shafts of criticism which give pungency and human interest to his celebrated book *Vom Kriege*. All of these advisers had acquired a kind of prescriptive right of submitting plans of campaign for the consideration of the whole Council on the smallest provocation, a fact- which the Duke of Brunswick rather favoured, as it tended to relieve him of responsibility, but which Hohenlohe and Massenbach resented most bitterly as the natural consequence was to restrain their initiative. This was gall and wormwood to the latter, who imagined himself chosen by Providence itself to rescue the Prussian Monarchy from its perilous position, not by straightforward fighting, but by a display of those higher arts of diplomacy and war (of which he fondly believed Napoleon to be entirely ignorant, a view very largely shared by many of his colleagues) of which he had always been the recognized spokesman.

Massenbach's idea of making a career had always been to attract attention by a display of versatility and of diplomatic talent. No event was allowed to escape without a contribution from his prolific pen; and he had always been an immense admirer of the principles of the Revolution and of Napoleon's career. Such admiration was considered in those days as the sign of an enlightened mind, and provided one kept within the bounds of respect and decency prescribed for an officer bearing the King of Prussia's Commission, such exuberance brought credit rather than the reverse. Ever since Marengo he had advocated an alliance with France as the best solution of the existing situation, and the idea at the back of his mind seems to have been that by making skilful use of the art of manoeuvre based on the theory of positions, above alluded to (two branches of the "Art of War" which Napoleon's practice clearly proved him to be ignorant of), a sufficiently satisfactory relation of the two Armies could be brought about, to justify mutual reconciliation after some trifling engagements "for the honour of the Arms." To arrange this it was absolutely necessary to oppose a *"non possumus"* attitude to all orders and suggestions from Headquarters, and as we shall presently see, it was his persistence in this attitude that brought about the final disasters of Jena and Prenzlau.

The orders for mobilization having been issued on August 9, three clear weeks before Napoleon began to make counter arrangements, it is somewhat startling to find that it was not until September 25 that the Duke of Brunswick submitted to the King his first plan of operations, which, as Clausewitz points out, would have been quite reasonable had it been presented and acted upon a fortnight earlier.

Clausewitz's criticisms on this plan have so often been presented in a truncated fashion, and so much misunderstood, that it is well worth while to give them here almost in *extenso*, as they are impregnated with the clearest commonsense and are founded on an accurate knowledge of the ground and all the circumstances.

> The question was, by which roads to move against the enemy. Should one
> (1) Leave the Thüringian Forest on the right and advance by Hof and its vicinity on Bamberg,
> (2) Leave it to the left, and move along the Frankfort road, or
> (3) Cross the forest and strike at Würzburg, or

(4) Separate and move in two, if not in three columns in all three directions.

The principal points to be considered in arriving at a decision were:—

(a) To keep together as much as possible, because concentration on the battlefield was the principal point.

(b) To strike an important fraction of the enemy's forces and destroy it—a victory over an inconsiderable portion of his Army would only give him time to concentrate the remainder and thus ensure a numerical preponderance.

Point a effectually excluded the idea of marching in more than one direction with the main Army.

Point b eliminated a move on Frankfurt, since in that district there lay only Augereau's Corps, which might very probably evade the blow by joining the bulk of the Army in Franconia.

There remained thus only the choice between the advance across the Thüringian Forest, or by Hof on Baireuth.

If Magdeburg and Wittenberg were taken as the principal lines of retreat, then one's communications would be best covered by the former, if Dresden were selected for retreat, then the latter was preferable. Undoubtedly, Magdeburg and Wittenberg were the better points on which to retreat, since they covered Berlin more directly, and the Elbe between these towns formed a more serious obstacle than about Dresden, whilst Silesia, with its numerous fortresses and sheltered position behind the Bohemian Mountains, could be safely left to take care of itself. These considerations should have sufficed for the choice of the advance through Thuringia, and besides on this line one was more in the centre of events and could meet a turning movement against the right better than from the line Hof to Baireuth.

Lastly, an offensive through the Forest District was more likely to disconcert the enemy, since owing to its relative roadlessness, this was the last direction likely to be selected (by an Army cumbered with heavy *impedimenta* understood).

In accordance with these ideas, the Duke proposed to move, ten Divisions in six columns through the Mountains to Meiningen and Hildburghausen, whence they were to advance to the attack, whilst one Division watched the country about Baireuth, and three Divisions (Rüchel's Command) remained facing Augereau towards Frankfurt.

These operations were to commence on October 9, and the troops were due to arrive on the line Meiningen-Hildburghausen at latest on the 11th, and though it was always possible that the enemy might intervene to prevent their realization, still that chance must always be taken in War, and one could always revert to the Defensive, for which case the following ideas were laid down.

If the enemy attacked before we were ready the Army was to concentrate backwards about Erfurt and Weimar. In this position one faced him directly whether he came along the great Frankfurt-Erfurt road or over the Thüringian Mountains. If he came through Baireuth and Hof, then we had the Saale between him and us, and if they tried to maintain their direction towards Leipzig and Dresden, we could anticipate them by a flank march at Weissenfels, whilst if they wheeled in to their left to cross the Saale and attack us, they offered us an opportunity for a counter attack under the best possible conditions, for the Valley of the Saale may here be characterized as a ravine, and the open plateaus to the north-west of it favoured to the utmost our conventional tactics.

The correctness of this appreciation is sufficiently demonstrated by the fact that when the last-named contingency actually arose, the Prussian Army was still able to bring 45,000 men on to the field of Auerstadt against 27,000 under Davout, and caught the latter in the most unfavourable conditions conceivable, with their backs against an almost insuperable physical obstacle. Of course it was a risk in face of an enemy superior both in numbers and energy of command, to remain so long in a flank position, the natural line of retreat from which lay in prolongation of its left flank, but if the worst came to the worst there was always a wide area of friendly country behind, whereas Bonaparte also had to form front to a flank, with the Bohemian frontier, anything but hospitable, only some twenty miles away to his rear.

This plan of the Duke's, which has always appeared to me both simple, natural, and founded on sound common sense, threw Hohenlohe and Massenbach into a perfect frenzy of rage.

They had already submitted their plans of campaign, (unsolicited, however well-intentioned,) to the King, (a step which reveals the spirit and tone of the two men), in accordance with which the Prince's Command was to be raised to six Divisions and to picket the passes and defiles of Saalfeld, Saalburg, Hof and Adorf, whilst the main Army was to move along the great road to Eisenach and Vach, and so, in continuation of its offensive, with two great masses, like wing bastions, to turn the Thüringian Forest, whilst 10,000 men held it occupied, and General von Rüchel on the right flank (presumably, therefore, in Hesse or in Eichsfeld) carried out an active defensive.[1]

These confused ideas emanating from Massenbach's inflamed brain have been almost universally adopted by contemporary writers as a basis for their criticisms, and almost in precise proportion to the more or less com-

---

[1] This is taken from a book by Rühle von Lilienstein, evidently inspired by Massenbach, entitled *Bericht eines Augenzeugen von des Feldzug dee Fürsten Hohenlohe* in 1806.Vol. i. p. 25.

prehension of the matters involved which they brought to bear on their subject. Some day, and let us hope soon, the conviction will prevail that the great movements and combinations of War must always be very simple, not only because complicated ones are difficult of execution, but because they involve generally useless roundabout movements, not leading directly to the purpose. Then people will see this *pedantry of the General Staff* in all its nakedness, whereby for more than a century Governments and Nations have been tormented. Then, too, people will marvel how it was possible for their ancestors to be so deceived by hollow phrases and false similes, such as "Wing Bastions "and "Active defensive," in such earnest matters, where only the utmost clearness and precision in expression are in place,—but enough of this indignation. The writer only gives way to it not to warn posterity, but to repel the possible insinuation that he himself ever succumbed to these delusions.

"As soon as the Prince and Massenbach learnt of the Duke's proposal, they were completely beside themselves, and believed that they were showing the utmost courtesy and discretion by *forbidding any member of their Staff to make fun of their Commander-in-Chief's imbecilities.* Since they realized that their own schemes were not likely to be formally accepted, they determined to involve the Duke in such measures that the force of accomplished facts would compel him to cross over to the right bank of the Saale.

A defensive position on the right bank of that river would, in fact, as a 'defensive measure,' have been at once more simple and natural, but the Duke's plan was based on the offensive, hence it was altogether wrong to endeavour to force the hand of the Commander, and thereby to increase the want of decision and confusion already apparent in the Army Headquarters, but the idea had become an obsession with both, and all Massenbach's energies henceforth were absorbed in this effort to compel the Duke to concentrate on the right bank of the river.

Already on October 4, however, whilst the Duke was in Weimar and the Army still in process of concentration, news arrived which made it extremely improbable that his plan of September 25 could be carried through without serious fighting. Bonaparte was reported at Aschaffenburg, and the bulk of his Army, it was afterwards ascertained, was on this date between Nürnberg-Schweinfurt, Bamberg and Hammelburg.

From this time forward the state of the Duke's mind became plain. He had always cherished the hope that War might yet be averted, and the secret intention to make use of the presence of the King with Headquarters, to unload his responsibility upon the latter's shoulders, and now instead of forming an independent resolution, as he would have had to do, in the King's absence, he availed himself of the circumstances to call a council for October 5, to decide what should next be undertaken.

On October 4 a preliminary meeting was held between the Duke, General Phull, Colonels Massenbach and Kleist, and Captain Müffling.

The Duke had, in fact, already given up the idea of an offensive in his own mind, though for the moment he kept this to himself, and maintained that he was convinced that Bonaparte would take up a position on the Upper Saale in order not to appear as the aggressor, and Massenbach reported the result of a reconnaissance in that region in order to strengthen his case for bringing the main body over to the right bank of the river.

This idea had now completely taken possession of his mind, and he talked unceasingly about it, *with the obstinacy of a refractory horse trying to crush his rider's leg against the riding-school wall.* But there was so little coherence in his thoughts, and it was so clearly evident that he himself was hardly conscious of their consequences, that he convinced no one, and all his efforts served only to increase the prevailing indecision.

On the 5th, the actual Council assembled, and besides His Majesty there were present: the Duke, Field Marshal von Möllendorf, Prince von Hohenlohe, General von Rüchel, General von Phull, General von Köckritz, and Colonels von Massenbach, von Scharnhorst, Kleist, and Grafs. Haugwitz and Luchesini.

Massenbach again urged the importance of crossing the Saale, and Scharnhorst, weary of this continuous divergence of opinion, and foreseeing the dangers which threatened us from its continuance, submitted that 'In War it was not so much what one did that mattered, but that whatever action was agreed upon should be carried out with unity and energy'.[1]

Hence, since there seemed no reasonable prospect of reaching an agreement between the views of Headquarters and those of Prince Hohenlohe, and further discussion would waste time, he proposed that the former should waive their objections and carry out the Prince's plan at once without further hesitation and delay. But Massenbach had done so little to convince the Council that even this proved of no avail.

Massenbach then suggested as an alternative a concentration in three groups, Rüchel, at Craula, between Eisenach, and Langensalza, the main Army at Erfurt, and Prince Hohenlohe at the Ettersberg, near Weimar, which grouping he considered a sufficient concentration. This proposal is abundant proof that even Massenbach was

---

1. This saying I translate literally, as it has since passed into a proverb in the German Army.

not sufficiently sure of his ground whether the French would advance through Franconia or not. If they did, then the only suitable position to meet them in would have been at Weimar, i.e., as near to the Saale as possible. But no agreement was come to, and the Council broke up to assemble again the same afternoon.

Then at length the decision was arrived at to continue the movements already in progress until the 8th, which was appointed as a day of rest for the troops, and meanwhile to send out reconnaisances from all three Armies, and reconnoitre in detail the proposed positions at Craula-Erfurt and near Blankenhaym (about 10 miles South of Weimar).

The King, however, condemned the reconnaissances, and only Captain Müffling was sent (presumably with an escort) towards the Upper Saale. His information could be in by the 8th, and then, if still advisable, the original movement through the Thüringen Forest could be commenced on October 9.

From henceforward the Duke of Brunswick appears in a very unfavourable light. As a man who feels he is not up to his work and can no longer master his cares and anxieties, and ends by entangling himself completely whilst seeking alternatives where none exist.

The idea of leaving to the decision of a congress of twelve persons what he himself might have settled by a single clear thought, the hope of averting the outbreak of War, the conception that the French would take up a defensive position in Franconia, show a complete want of judgment; but the Duke, nevertheless, was by no means wanting in that faculty, and would not have shown such indecision had he only stood alone. But accustomed to conceal his own opinions and submit to the guidance of his official superiors, and surrounded by men, evidently there to supervise his conduct, he felt constrained, partly by policy, partly by duty, to keep himself in the background in order not to enhance his responsibility, in the event of misfortune, by having wished to appear wiser than his councillors.

Thus perished what yet remained of decision and clearness of thought in the mind of the seventy year old veteran, through the friction resulting from the thoroughly unmilitary constitution of the organ of Chief Command.

The position of the Prussian Army on October 6th was neither involved nor even dangerous. If it was no longer possible to count on a strategic surprise, the only thing to be done was to fall back frankly on the advantages the 'Defensive' form affords and make the most of them, i.e., wait for the enemy's advance through Saxony in order either to attack him one's self, or select a strong position which he could not afford to pass by, which therefore he would himself have to assail, or finally, in case he appeared altogether too strong to risk a decisive action, then to retreat step by step into the interior in order to collect reinforcements. To attack him offered no chance of success, unless one had the luck to find him divided, and that was no more likely to occur in Saxony than during his passage through Franconia, the chance that had already been thrown away. Hence it only remained to take up a position which would afford opportunities to combine the defensive with the offensive, and attack out of it in full force as soon as the enemy passed within striking radius.

To retreat without a battle would only be justifiable if the enemy showed numbers altogether beyond hope of our defeating. This was not yet certain; hence, since the decision whether to attack, defend, or retreat depended on circumstances still to be discovered, there was nothing further to be done for the moment than to wait, as we actually did, about the centre of the theatre of operations, and reconnoitre a suitable position for a decisive battle.

Here there was an alternative to be considered. The Saale flows in a deep and rocky ravine, and thus divides the district into two areas with very different topographical features.

If we chose a position on the left bank of the river, then we faced the enemy coming up through the Thüringian Forest directly, and covered equally directly our lines of retreat upon Magdeburg and Wittenberg; on the other hand, if the enemy came up through Saxony from Baireuth, we could only oppose a flanking position to his advance.

On the right bank, however, though we opposed the enemy's advance through Saxony directly—with lines of retreat to Leipzig and Dresden—we could not take up a flanking position against him if he came by way of the Thüringian Forest or from Eisenach, because the Bohemian frontier was then far too close behind us — and the least threat at our right flank would compel us to evacuate the position on pain of being thrown back upon the Bohemian mountains if defeated, and thus severed from the whole of our national resources. The enemy could therefore drive us back over the Elbe without risking an engagement merely by out marching us. But on the left bank of the Saale the conditions were quite different. Here we had the whole of North Germany behind us, and in *case of necessity* could retreat in any direction. We underline, *in case of necessity,* because we do not wish to underrate the importance of remaining in communication with the Oder and with Prussia.

Hence, since we could not risk the passage of the Saale ravine at the last moment in face of the enemy, a timely choice on which side of the river to make our stand was absolutely imperative.

As long as we remained in uncertainty as to whether the enemy was coming by Eisenach, the Thüringian Forest or by Hof, the position on the left bank of the Saale was the most central and, therefore, preferable. But as soon as we knew positively that the weight of the attack was coming from the south, it could only be considered as a flanking position, though one of quite unusual strength.

The first condition of a flanking position is that the enemy should not be able to evade it, but must wheel up and attack it. This condition is very seldom fulfilled, but in this case it was completely satisfied, for the width between the Saale and the Bohemian frontier is so inconsiderable, and the French communications passed so near to the river bank, that it was impossible for them to march along the front of the Prussians in position, and hence a battle became unavoidable.[1]

The second condition is that it should offer tactical advantages to the side which holds it. Now the left bank of the Saale offered the most favourable ground conceivable for the Prussian tactics, whilst the few passages across the ravine formed by the river could be held by our light troops for a comparatively long period of time, hence our main body held together in a central position, could fall upon that portion of the enemy's forces which first exposed itself to a blow.

The enemy would therefore be compelled to fight with his back against a precipitous ravine with no room for deployment, and the Bohemian Mountains in his rear, whilst his communications ran out sideways along the river. *In fact, in all history there is scarcely an instance to be found of a similarly advantageous position for an Army compelled to assume the defensive.*[2]

---

1. This paragraph is additional proof that Clausewitz, even twenty years after the War, had still failed to grasp the inherent strength of the Napoleonic conception.
2. Compare also Clausewitz *On War.* Book vi, chap, xxviii.

Thus Erfurt was indicated as a preliminary position. Thence we could meet directly any enemy approaching from Eisenach or the Thüringian Forest, and concentrate upon one of his columns with crushing superiority. Or, if he came up through Saxony, then we could move to Weimar and occupy the passages of the Saale.

If the enemy then attempted to march across our front, which was hardly conceivable, then covered by the Saale we could move in perfect safety by the great road to Merseburg and head him off at or near that point. Very few arrangements, e.g., a pair of pontoon bridges at Freiburg, and the occupation of Kosen and Merseburg would suffice to ensure the success of this project, which would have been quite normal and prudent; or we might, if we had the courage, cross the Saale behind him and attack him so that he would have no retreat open but into Bohemia. Such a bold step would have been justified by the mutual relations of the b'nes of communication, for whereas the enemy would have had none except into Bohemia open to him, we retained the passages of the Saale and all North Germany behind us. Bonaparte in such a position would not have hesitated for a moment to have dealt his enemy the most crushing blow conceivable in War. But in face of the superiority of the enemy, both moral and material, and with the admitted weakness of our supreme command, such a stroke was hardly to be expected.[1]

---

1. It will be seen in the following chapters how completely the Napoleonic form provided for this very danger. Yet, viewing Jena as a whole, and not only a single step in the campaign, its boldness gave it the best chance of success. The Prussians had as yet no right to consider themselves beaten, and it was always more than possible that, say, 100,000 Prussians might have so completely shattered the covering force immediately opposed to them that the moral of the main Army might have broken down for ever, under Napoleon, psychological panics were neither impossible nor unknown.

Scharnhorst had indeed advocated it, in case the opportunity arose, but the Duke declined to consider it.

If, instead of trying to march across our front, the enemy wheeled in to the left to attack us, then we had all the above-mentioned advantages on our side in the ensuing battle. This is indeed what actually happened, and the result justifies our contention. The Duke of Brunswick with 45,000 men struck Davout on October 14, at the head of 27,000 and he might just as well, had he stood fast on the 13th, have had 80,000 men to hurl against Bonaparte on the 14th, who had only 60,000 at his disposal, he would then have had 25,000 still in hand to keep the passages at Kosen, Camburg and Dornburg against Davout, Murat and Bernadotte.

If, therefore, we renounced the Offensive, the decision to be taken on October 6 was quite simple, *viz.*, to leave Tauenzien at Hof as a corps of observation, with instructions to withdraw towards Naumburg without allowing himself to be drawn into a serious engagement. To occupy the passages of the Saale from Saalburg to Jena, and to place Hohenlohe behind Jena. Rüchel and the main Army about Erfurt with outposts towards the Thüringian Forest and Eisenach.

The measures which were actually adopted were not very different, and we might, in spite of everything, have looked forward to the battle of October 14 without much anxiety had not—

    1. General Tauenzien lost too heavily in his retreat from Hof, and taken the direction of Jena, thus leaving Naumburg and Kosen unoccupied and allowing the enemy to press forward along the Leipzig road unhindered and unobserved.

    2. Prince Louis been completely defeated, a consequence of an entirely uncalled-for act of daring.

3. Hohenlohe's Army been struck with panic, to which point we will recur later.

4. The Duke of Brunswick made the mistake of sending the Duke of Weimar into the Thüringian Forest.

Thanks to these four errors, the Army went into battle 20,000 men weaker than it should have been and much shaken in its confidence. But these mistakes had nothing to do with the earlier plans, and two of them were due to the faults of subordinates and cannot thus be charged upon the shoulders of the Duke.

Certainly, these advantages of our position, revealed by the above investigation, depended for their realization on an Army which knew how to fight and on leaders with determination enough to seize their opportunities, and at the time these qualities we all believed to be abundantly present both in the troops and our principal commanders. Had it been possible to forecast the want of skill shown in action, the indecision and lack of council of our leaders, the mass of insubordination, the confusion and contradiction which events actually disclosed, then the only rational course to have pursued would have been to take up a position square across the Leipzig road so as at least to have retained the possibility of running away.

In spite of all these delays, the positions which the various sections of the Prussian Army actually occupied on October 6 were well adapted to the actual situation as Clausewitz frankly admits. It was only the *moral* of the Staff that suffered from these interminable discussions, and the want of controlling power which they revealed.

The Saxons around Roda with their scouts watching the exits from the mountains were well placed to give timely information of the French approach, and all that was necessary to meet the situation which actually arose was to concentrate, designedly, around Weimar and Apolda, whilst observing by detachments the several passages of the Saale. In fact, the positions actually occupied on October 11 could hardly have been improved upon (as subsequent comments will show) had they been deliberately selected by the exercise of the free will of the Commander and not forced upon him as a consequence of unforeseen events.

But the nerves of the directing organ were in no condition to stand the shock of the news of the French invasion when at length it arrived, and instead of coolly and deliberately occupying the flanking position of unusual strength which the defile of the Saale supplied, the various detachments swarmed like bees from a hive, and only drifted into the positions they eventually occupied on the day before the battle, as the result of a succession of orders, counter-orders, and disorder, and of two partial engagements which, taken altogether, produced profound demoralization and drove the Saxons to the very verge of mutiny. In detail their movements were as follows—

On the evening of October 6 the main body of the Saxons lay about Roda,, with a strong advance guard near Hof, close to the Bavarian frontier. Hohenlohe's command lay widely distributed in the triangle Erfurt, Jena, Saalfeld and the principal Army, between Eisenach, Gotha and Langensalza; Rüchel and Blücher being near Eisenach, but on the whole to the westward, with advance parties towards Fulda.

During the 7th the principal Army merely corrected its positions, moving towards the Eisenach-Gotha road; and Hohenlohe commenced to concentrate his troops towards the Saale in case it should become necessary to cross to the right bank of that river.

Tauenzien, finding himself in presence of a strong French column (Soult's Advance Guard) withdrew skirmishing on Schleiz, calling in also his detachment from Saalburg. The Saxons remained in their position about Roda.

On the morning of the 8th Capt. Müffling's report from Meiningen arrived. He had received trustworthy news of Napoleon's advance in three great columns through the Thüringian forest towards Saxony, and had been informed that the French were marching in a most unmilitary manner, i.e. without advance or flank guards, and straggling considerably—which was, in fact, the case, as the marches his informants had observed were only marches of concentration, and Napoleon had not yet considered it necessary to fatigue his men by tactical precautions or rigid discipline. Müffling's report concluded with a proposal to send an expedition of 10 to 15 squadrons to take advantage of this laxity, and this suggestion, though sound in itself, was one of the principal causes which led to the defeat of the whole Army on the 14th.

It appealed so strongly to the Duke of Brunswick that he immediately conceived the idea of extending the principle, and actually ordered the despatch of small columns of all arms (because Cavalry unsupported was held to be of little use in such forest-clad and hilly country), aggregating in all some 12,500 men, not only through Meiningen, but further west *via* Fulda, Hammelburg on Würzburg. The essence, however, of Müffling's proposal had been the despatch of a rapidly moving column of horsemen to break in upon the French communications in the open country beyond the mountains—an operation which the Prussian Cavalry of to-day would not hesitate to undertake.[1]

On the same day (the 8th) the Duke of Brunswick ordered the Strategic Reserve under the Duke of Würtemberg from Magdeburg to Halle; Hohenlohe halted his troops for a day's rest; the Saxons also remained at Roda, and Tauenzien reached Schleiz.

---

1. In the manoeuvres of 1892, at which I was present, the Cavalry of the XIth Corps, starting from Cassel, crossed the same range at its western extremity, and marching sixty and fifty miles on two consecutive days, flooded the plains about Mühlhausen and Langensalza without in the least impairing their efficiency. See *Marching through Thuringia,* in my Military Essays, etc.

October 9th. Early in the morning a report from Prince Louis at Saalfeld reached Hohenlohe, notifying the advance of the French through Grafenthal during the previous day; and Hohenlohe hastened to send off orders for his troops to concentrate along the Saale from Rudolstadt to Kahla, ready to cross the river next morning if necessary. Meanwhile a detachment was sent forward to Neustadt to cover the retreat of Tauenzien, who had been ordered to continue his withdrawal from Schleiz to that place.

But owing to the usual friction at all the Headquarter offices of the day, the orders did not reach their destination in time for the movement to be completed, and many battalions, after being under arms all day, were compelled to march far into the night to reach their allotted positions. It seems also that in the prevailing confusion no one had thought of a technical reconnaissance of the river itself, for some engineers were detailed to draw up a report on the existing fords and facilities for crossing, on the 10th and 11th.

Of the principal Army, Rüchel concentrated round Gotha: Blücher was still north-east of Eisenach, and the Duke of Weimar's detachment extended along the road from Gotha to Schweinfurt, with its head in Meiningen, its tail in Schmalkalden. The main body itself drew a little closer round Erfurt.

Meanwhile Tauenzien had been severely handled by the advance guard of the Central French Column (which under Bernadotte was coming up from Lobenstein through Saalburg), and was retreating in considerable disorder towards Neustadt. On this day the troops under Hohenlohe first began to suffer from hunger. The Saxons seem never to have known anything else.

October 10th. The news of Tauenzien's defeat at Schleiz received during the afternoon of the 9th (hour not now discoverable) at length compelled Hohenlohe to make up his mind, and he now determined to cross the Saale next morning at all costs in order to occupy a position about Neustadt and Mittel Pölllnitz together with the Saxons already near Roda.

In the evening he despatched a Staff Officer, Capt. von Valentini, to Prince Louis, who with the main body of the advance guard occupied Rudolstadt. The Prince had already received information of the approach of the French left Column (Lannes) from Grafenthal, and concluded that it was his duty to hinder the enemy from debouching from the mountains as long as possible in order to gain time for the main body under Hohenlohe to file across his rear and join the Saxons at Neustadt. Unfortunately he failed to notice that whereas from Kahla or Orlamünde to Neustadt is barely 10 miles, from Saalfeld to Neustadt is over 20, and Grafenthal, where the French were reported, is another 15. There was therefore no occasion for him to trouble about Hohenlohe's movement at all—distance alone was a sufficient protection for it. However, he took the opposite view, with consequences most disastrous both for himself and the whole Army. He marched to Saalfeld with every available battalion (*viz.* 10 battalions, 10 squadrons, and 2½ batteries), and meeting Lannes at the head of the V Corps, was completely outfought by the French veterans. Prince Louis himself was killed, and his troops completely dispersed, whilst the news of this disaster spread absolute consternation throughout the whole Army; for public opinion had long before elected the Prince as the coming man of the Prussian Army, and as this opinion was shared by Clausewitz also, it must have been based on some substantial foundation of fact.[1]

Prince Hohenlohe meanwhile was on his way from Kahla to Neustadt, distance 10 miles; he is alleged to have started at 3 a.m., but only reached the latter place about noon. Here he first heard the thunder of the guns at Saalfeld, and began to meet the remnants of Tauenzien's command beaten the

---

1. The actual losses were 29 officers, and about 1,700 men—killed and wounded—and 34 guns; but there were also many stragglers. and some of the battalions engaged were only able to form up 400 to 450 men three days later. See *Lettow Vorbeck,* vol. i, p. 245.

previous day at Schleiz. From these he learnt the extent of their disaster, which he had not previously realized, and at the same time news arrived that the French Cavalry were pressing closely in pursuit.

Under these circumstances the position at Neustadt appeared too exposed, so he ordered the Saxons back to Roda, and for himself rode back to Kahla, where he and his Staff settled down to their dinner still in ignorance of Prince Louis' fate.

About sundown a personal servant of Prince Louis arrived, bearing the official news of the defeat at Saalfeld and the Prince's death. The blow was for the moment overwhelming, for people had begun to forget that death and wounds were not unusual where guns were thundering. The orders forthwith issued as a consequence will hardly bear analysis. General Grawert, whose troops had been struggling with the difficulties of the ground since early morning and had been on their legs most of the previous night, were counter-marched and ordered back from the points they had reached on their way to Neustadt, through Orlamünde to Rudolstadt, to rally the fugitives. The Saxons were to continue their retreat from Roda to Jena, and the remainder of the command were also withdrawn to Kahla and Lobeda, whilst under the impression that the French were about to outmarch them altogether and cut them off from Halle and Dessau, Massenbach was sent back to the Duke's Headquarters at Blankenhayn to propose a concentration of the whole Army on the Ettersberg north of Weimar, Massenbach, however, crossed an order of the Duke's already on its way directing a somewhat similar movement, *viz.*, a concentration of the principal Army on Weimar, and of Prince Hohenlohe's command on Jena.

The Headquarters had, in fact, already taken alarm at the sound of the distant cannonade at Saalfeld. The troops were actually marching to their appointed positions in the usual peace time formations when the first guns were heard, and immediately Staff officers were galloping about like bees, endeavouring to arrange some more military order; and orders were hurriedly sent out to recall the Duke of Weimar's detachment from Meiningen,[1] and to hasten the movement of Blücher and Rüchel on Gotha and Erfurt respectively, with a view to the ultimate concentration of the whole force about Weimar, covered by Prince Hohenlohe at Jena.

October 11th. The above orders, however, for the most part only reached their destinations during the night, and the commencement of their execution had therefore to be delayed till daylight on the following morning. Rüchel and Blücher throwing their customary energy into their tasks marched over 30 miles each, and actually reached the western outskirts of Weimar during the night of the 11th. The remaining three Divisions which constituted the main body of the principal Army took up a camp at Umpferstedt, about 3 miles east of Weimar, but though no portions of the commands had more than about 13 miles to march, many failed to arrive before dark, and as no arrangements for wood, straw and food had been made, they passed a most uncomfortable night. The Cavalry were dispersed amongst the villages, but as the boundary separating the two Armies had not been precisely defined, they spread too far to the eastward, and according to Lettow Vorbeck (p. 274) they drove out the troops which had fought at Saalfeld, and had been sent under cover by Prince Hohenlohe's Staff to obtain rest after their sufferings. They even occupied Capellendorf, the village reserved for the Prince's Headquarters, and it took all his personal authority to induce them to clear out again. The front of the camp lay parallel to the Jena-Weimar road, i.e. faced about south-west, although nine-tenths of the Staff and the whole of the rank and file were by this time convinced that the enemy had

---

1. His advance squadrons had actually crossed the mountains and ridden up to within a few miles of Schweinfurt without, however, finding any enemy to attack. *Lettow Vorbeck*, p. 272.

outflanked them to the east and north. The Duke of Weimar on receipt of the order of recall decided very wisely to return *via* Ilmenau as the shortest way to rally the main body, but only arranged for a. ten mile march.

Prince Hohenlohe changed his Headquarters from Kahla to Jena, and the whole of the morning was taken up in disentangling the confusion of the previous evening and in reviewing and encouraging the Saxons who had fought at Saalfeld.

It had been decided to form a camp on the plateau north of Jena, and about noon the troops were filing through the narrow streets under the eyes of the Prince, when a sudden panic arose. It was alleged afterwards that as the head of the column cleared the town it was met by an excited Hussar with a bloodstained bandage round his head, who came galloping down the road *from* Weimar shouting, "Get back! get back! the

French are upon us." Be this as it may, the head of the column did check; some guns were sharply reversed and galloped back upon the Infantry in the crowded street, and in a few moments the panic spread throughout the whole town and up the valley as far as Lobeda. Some Saxon supply wagons coming from Neustadt actually turned round and never stopped in their flight until they were arrested by the real enemy in their efforts to escape from an imaginary one. Their contents, doubtless, formed a welcome addition to their captors' rather scanty cuisine.

Some hours elapsed before order could be restored on the Saale, and the march to the intended camp resumed; but it was never reached, as darkness soon closed down, and the worn-out men, now constantly under arms for three days and two nights, fell away by the roadside and slept when and where they could. This was perhaps fortunate, as Massenbach, in his efforts to perform Scharnhorst's duties as well as his own, had entirely forgotten to see to the laying out of the camp, his first duty as Quarter-Master-General!

Panics have occurred in all Armies, in all ages, and will continue to arise from time to time in the future; and it is a pity that as a rule such incidents are suppressed as much as possible, for their causation deserves the closest study, as it sheds unusual light upon the whole question of the "psychology of crowds," which in turn forms the scientific basis of all systems of military training.

In this instance the men had been subjected to the longest and severest drill training that perhaps the world has ever known; but this had been almost exclusively in relatively small units, and even on the manoeuvre grounds confusion had never even been simulated. As a consequence it had never dawned upon the regimental officers or the men that the best of Staffs are liable to error, and that confusion is in the very nature of War. An Army less uniform in the excellence of its fighting discipline would have taken the incidents of the marches and counter-marches far more philosophically. If a weak unit, here and there, had given way, the others would have pulled themselves together and jeered at the runaways, assisting also to stop them in their career and restore order. But here the distrust had been spreading downwards for days as each rank in succession realized the incompetence in the directing organs, and after three days and two nights of almost ceaseless marching and counter-marching, without even seeing the enemy, the individual minds were all tuned up to that key of expectancy of evil where a chance incident is sufficient to provoke a rupture. It is perhaps the most dramatically complete incident in history, for only a few moments before the very men with whom the panic originated had just marched past their commanding General, and the runaways actually precipitated themselves upon their comrades who were still defiling before him.

Its extent and completeness should also be noted, for without appreciating its magnitude, the paralysis which overcame the whole Army for the next twenty-four hours can hardly be understood.

October 12th. The issue of fresh provisions, and of firewood in particular, would have gone further to steady the growing feeling of unrest in the troops than perhaps any other measure, but nothing so practical seems to have entered the minds of the Prussian Commanders. Massenbach spent the whole morning in laying out a camp, and then the men moved in and pitched tents during the afternoon. It appears that the news of the fight at Saalfeld had led him to conclude that the enemy would cross to the left bank of the Saale, hence the camp was formed in order of battle facing south-west, with open ground most suitable for the Prussian tactics in its front. But, unfortunately, the French were marching on the right bank as fast as they could and were already approaching Naumburg, well in the Prussian rear. On inquiry it was discovered that the officers' patrols ordered by the Duke to be sent out on the right bank on the previous morning had been overlooked, and no one had the slightest idea as to where the enemy really was. All this time it appears Massenbach was doing Scharnhorst's duty as well as his own, and the latter was kept at a distance by the whole of his official superiors. In the afternoon the advance guard of Marshal Lannes appeared to the South of Jena, causing fresh panic in the town, but this was dealt with by a small contingent on the spot, who moved out, and engaged the enemy at the village of Winzerle, and held him till nightfall. This little alert brought this advantage in its train that at last the men on the spot took action on their own initiative, and a line of outposts was supplied, facing south and east along the river. It was well that these subordinates at least had kept their heads, for meanwhile a rumour of the occupation of Naumburg reached Headquarters shortly after midday, which effectually caused the latter to lose theirs.

At length an officer of the Military Train arrived and reported that he had been driven out of that town by the French. To clear up the situation, a couple of squadrons were ordered off to reconnoitre, the King himself instructed their commander, and they were about to start, when a civilian turned up who asserted that Naumberg was not in the hands of the enemy. In accordance with the spirit of the times the loose assertion of the civilian was allowed to override the positive testimony of the officer, and the squadrons were sent back to their regiments.

Finally at 11 p.m. definite confirmation of the presence of the French in that town was received, and the news spread consternation everywhere.

A council was at once summoned for the following morning. Rüchel from Weimar, about seven miles away, was ordered to attend, and Hohenlohe was told to send Massenbach. (Lettow Vorbeck, p. 306). What time it actually assembled is uncertain, but the-decision to retreat on the Elbe via Freiburg and Taucha, in order to pick up the Duke of Wurtemberg's Reserve at Halle, appears to have been reached in time enough to allow of Scharnhorst issuing the necessary orders about 10 a.m. The actual text of these orders has not been preserved, but Prince Hohenlohe's recollection of them, handed in with his defence before the Commission of Inquiry in 1808 is accepted by Lettow Vorbeck as authentic.

The Army marches off on the 13th, with intervals of two hours between successive Divisions, towards Auerstadt. On the 14th, after having cooked, one Division will be advanced to cover the defile of Kösen, the remainder will file off left in front behind it to the bridge at Freiburg, where they will cross the Unstrut, and take up a position on the heights beyond, the right wing on the Unstrut, the front along the Saale.

The Reserve under General Kalckreuth moves at the same time, also left in front, passes the Unstrut at Laucha and encamps there.

General Rüchel moves from Erfurt by Weimar to the Lehnstedter heights and takes up the position evacuated by the Army. The Duke of Weimar will rejoin and maintain communication between the Corps of General Rüchel and Prince Hohenlohe.

Prince Hohenlohe will remain in his present position, but will detach during the 13th a sufficient body to Dornburg and Camburg to ensure the security of the march of the main body.[1]

October 13th. Returning now to the actual events amongst the Prussian troops on this day. The morning brought fresh and grave anxiety to Prince Hohenlohe, for the Saxon Commander, his men being worn out by want of food and disgusted with the total want of arrangements made for their comfort, sent a formal notice to the Prince by a body of representative officers, announcing his intention to secede from the Alliance and to march his men back to Dresden. The complaints were well founded in fact, for the men had practically received no food issues for four days and had borne more than their share of the marching and fighting. Moreover, the blame undoubtedly did rest on the Prussian Commissariat, and the Prince admitted the fact, and had indeed already complained personally to the King, but no remedial measure had as yet been taken.

His situation, had the Saxons carried out their threat, would have been desperate indeed, but fortunately he met the deputation with much tact and forbearance, and his own good will was so apparent that the mutineers gave up their point, on the Prince's promising that the Prussians should share what bread they had with their comrades, and assigning to them a district for foraging and requisitioning, which was in those days a most unheard-of responsibility to as-

---

1. These orders certainly do not bear the imprint of Scharnhorst's genius, for though it were vain to look for the accurate form in use in the present day in any orders of that date, a more confusing document it would be hard to find. In what order were the Divisions to march? at what time to start, surely the time was of more importance than the instruction "left in front."

sume. The report dealing with this circumstance given by Lettow Vorbeck, and derived from the War Office Archives in Berlin, is too long to reproduce in *extenso*, but it deserves the attention of all serious students, as it is typical of the state of military minds in Germany at that period. It is scarcely credible that in such a crisis the Prince should have found it necessary to contradict the rumour that Prussia and France had entered into a secret treaty to divide and plunder Saxony between them (Lettow Vorbeck, p. 326).

Whilst these negotiations between the Commanders were in progress, General Tauenzien was withdrawing from the line of outposts he had held during the night; but though skirmishing fire had continued till early morning, when the usual autumnal morning fog put a stop to it, this withdrawal was effected in the same casual manner, as if in deepest peace time. Fortunately the French did not perceive their opportunity, and ultimately a long line of pickets was thrown out from the Isserstedter Forest along the crest of the slopes overlooking the Landgrafenberg to the copses about Closewitz, and here about 10.30 a.m. the French took up the contact they had lost, and Lannes notified the presence of the enemy to the Emperor.

Hohenlohe, riding through his camp, about Capellendorf, to satisfy himself as to the spirit of the men, hearing the firing and being received with enthusiasm by the men of Grawert's Division, called for forty volunteers from each battalion (10 a.m.), and placing himself at their head rode out towards the Dornburg, the culminating point of the plateau, intending to give them a little occupation and amusement for the moment. On the way, as the firing grew heavier, he sent for the whole of the Reserve Infantry, two Prussian and two Saxon Cavalry Regiments and two horse batteries, and rallying some small detachments on this compact little force he advanced, men and officers in the highest spirits at the hope of at length coming to close quarters with their hitherto mysterious enemy.

This, I take it, was the crisis of the whole campaign, for

Lannes's Advance Guard would have been crushingly out-numbered, and had the Landgrafenberg been reoccupied, the whole course of events must have been changed. Undoubt-edly it would have been recaptured next morning, but hardly until the fog had lifted, and this must have delayed the deci-sion of the following day to so late an hour, that the main body would again have effected its junction with Hohenlohe on its retreat from Auerstadt, and the yet intact troops of the two forces would have made good their retreat to Magde-burg,–under conditions which would effectually have pre-cluded the wholesale disorganization and surrenders which actually took place.

At this moment Massenbach returned from Headquarters with the orders to which I have already referred, and a verbal message from the Duke of Brunswick, sent by authority of the King, that no serious engagement with the enemy was to be entered into that day.[1]

The Prince was furious on receipt of this message, but there was nothing for it but to obey, and as at the same mo-ment a rumour arrived that the enemy had occupied Dorn-burg, a village in the valley of the Saale about 5 miles be-low Jena, which he had been specially cautioned to retain, he marched his little command in that direction, although fighting there even would equally have entailed a breach of his instructions.

After the event, when it had become clear that the oc-cupation of the Landgrafenberg was in fact vital, more was made of this incident than it really merits. Lettow Vorbeck has gone into all the evidence with most painstaking care, and has concluded that at the moment the real cause of the

---

1. It has often been suggested, notably by Hopfner, that Massenbach invented this most unfortunate message. This, however, has been since disproved by the discovery of an independent record by another Staff Officer from Headquar-ters, von Boyen, who was sent off by the Duke about noon with a precisely similar message.

Prince's rage was not for the lost opportunities of observation and defence that the possession of the Landgrafenberg would have afforded, but was simply due to his disgust at losing the opportunity for a brilliant little bit of fighting. All we know of his character seems to confirm this supposition, and reasoning on the ordinary characteristics of human nature displayed in our own and many other armies all over the world, I am convinced that this explanation is the correct one. The Prince wanted a fight badly, and seeing a loophole of escape in his instructions about Dornburg, he marched thither at once, the idea of the importance of the Landgrafenberg never having presented itself to his mind, any more than it had done to any other man on the ground, for its value was *"nil per se"* but only accrued from the special use that Napoleon, by his own particular methods, was able to make of it. It was utterly inconceivable to the tacticians of the Frederickian school that 60,000 men could make their way up its utmost inaccessible sides and thence drive a hole through their whole line of battle. They wanted to get the enemy out into the open, not to prevent his coming, and had they had a fair numerical strength on the spot next day, with a real leader to command them, the result would have justified their preconceptions.

This, however, is in anticipation of events, and we must return to the troops now on the march towards Dornburg. The rumour which had set them in motion, to the effect that a French command had ordered food to be prepared for 12,000 men, no doubt, acted as a spur to these hungry soldiers, and "singing gaily," the little corps reached the heights above the village about 5 p.m., but nothing was to be seen of the enemy, though fortunately the provisions were ready, and willing volunteers soon carried them up the hill to their comrades. After this very unexpected picnic had been enjoyed, a few cavalry pickets were left about Dornburg and Camburg, and the remainder distributed over wide cantonments. The Prince returned to his Headquarters and his dinner, which we are told passed off very pleasantly, thanks to the company of an important French Staff Officer who had been taken prisoner, and with whom the Prince was pleased to renew a former acquaintance.

In the meanwhile the principal Army, in obedience to the orders, had moved off, about noon, all five Divisions on a single road, with the consequence that they did not reach their camping-ground till far into the night, and then having received no food issues, serious disorder arose, and they plundered the surrounding villages, (even Auerstadt, the Royal Headquarters, not escaping,) with serious consequences on the following morning.

Schmettau's Division, which led the march, (the light troops under Blücher being employed to cover the exposed flank,) took six hours to cover 13 miles, and though he had twenty squadrons at his disposal, so little thought was in those days devoted to reconnaissance that the only useful information sent in came from an officer's patrol despatched towards Naumburg which reported that Davout was in occupation of Kösen with 16,000 men. All along their march brisk outbursts of musketry had been heard on the right flank, arising from collisions between French scouts and Blücher's light troops, but these appear to have attracted little attention, and it was only on receipt of this news from Naumburg that Headquarters appear to have realized the coming danger, and prepared for it by sending the Queen—who had hitherto accompanied her husband, and in the opinion of her contemporaries, had been worth many additional battalions—back to Weimar. But instead of ordering Schmettau to press forward at all costs and block the exit from the Kösen defile, he was actually halted short of his original objective and only a few scouts were despatched towards the front.

Incredible though this oversight appears to us nowadays, it must again be insisted on that it was an almost necessary consequence of the tactical views of the day. The strength of the Prussian "line" lay in attack and a clear field of view and fire, and it was only the accident of the morning fog which disconcerted the legitimate anticipations of its leaders.

Speaking generally, over the whole of Northern Europe a commander is always in a better position to counter an enemy's designs when at the foot of a long gentle incline than at its summit; for whereas from the summit the convexity of the slope will almost invariably give cover to his enemy's reserves, from the foot, or near it, there must always be some sky line, against which approaching troops are certain to disclose themselves; and with the limited range of the weapons then in use this principle applied even more than nowadays.

Chapter 4

French Movements to October 13th

The Treaty of Pressburg, signed on December 25, 1805, having brought the war with Austria to a close, the Grand Army was at once withdrawn from Austrian territory, and distributed over wide cantonments throughout Southern Germany, where it lived at the cost of its Allies, and, as mentioned in the preceding chapter, from February 14 until September 5, only one letter, dated July 11, and having reference to a possible renewal of hostilities with Austria, was sent to it by the Emperor.

By September 5 the mobilisation orders for the Prussian Army had already been out for twenty-five days, but all this first letter contains is a request that Marshal Berthier, who had been left in chief command, should send in a report on the readiness for the field of the Army in his charge.[1]

Bonnal points out that, though left in this complete isolation, Berthier had no corresponding degree of initiative, but on the contrary was hampered by the following paragraph in the final letter of February 14.

"Keep strictly to the orders I give you, and execute punctually your instructions; every one must be ready and remain at his post; I alone know what I have to do." It would have needed a stronger character than Berthier's to have trans-

---

1. Bonnal, *La Manoeuvre de Jena*, p. 3.

gressed an order couched in such uncompromising terms. Needless to add Berthier did not even attempt to exceed the letter of his instructions, and the subsequent conduct of the campaign was not facilitated by his inaction.

The distribution of the troops during this period was as follows—The IV Corps (Soult) as covering force against the Austrians, The VII Corps (Augereau) against Hesse and the 2nd Division V Corps (Lannes) at Schweinfurt against the Prussians, backed by the bulk of the 1st (Bernadotte) about Ansbach, whilst the VI (Ney) was in reserve at Memingen[1]; the whole being able to concentrate either to the north or east within eight days of the receipt of orders to move.

To economise the resources of the country to the utmost, the units were widely disseminated within the district allotted to each command, and according to Fezensac (then a lieutenant in the 59th Foot, forming part of the VI Corps) his Brigade was only brought together once, for a review, during the whole period. The battalion commanders rarely visited the companies, and all the instructions the troops were given was such practice in company drill as their captains chose to impart.

The soldiers received neither pay nor clothes, and in reply to complaints, the commanders were told to help themselves as best they could. "This is how we managed," says the same authority. "At first the inhabitants gave each soldier a small bottle of wine a day. The captains asked to have its value in money instead, on condition that their hosts should no longer be called on to supply the wine. The money thus obtained was used to purchase trousers, of which we stood in great need, but somehow or other the men still received the wine." As for the higher officers they requisitioned everything they wanted, carriages and even banquets at the expense of the municipalities, and sixty years afterwards, as the writer can vouch from

---

1. South of Ulm, not to be confounded with Meiningen in the Thuringian Forest.

personal recollection, the survivors of those days had not forgotten these bitter experiences. One can only marvel at the extraordinary restraint their descendants exercised, when in 1870 the opportunity to pay off old scores arrived.[1]

Returning now to Napoleon's letters, two in number, of September 5. The first announces only the dispatch of 50,000 conscripts of 1806, soon to be followed by 30,000 of the reserve. The second orders the dispatch of Engineer officers to reconnoitre the roads from Bamberg to Berlin, about which he appears to have been but ill informed, as the following quotation suggests "They tell me there is a place called Torgau—is it fortified? " etc. Surely his perusal of the history of the Seven Years' War should have left him in little doubt on that point! He then continues:

> Eight days after I give the order, all my 'Armies,' that of Frankfort (VII Corps) that of Passau (IV Corps) that of Memingen (VI Corps) must be united at Bamberg and in the principality of Bayreuth. Send me the itinerary for each and the nature of the roads they must take. I suppose Soult will march by Straubing, Ney by Donauwerth, and Augereau by Würzburg. I conceive that in eight days all my *Corps d'armee* should be assembled beyond Kronach. Now from this point on the frontier of Bamberg to Berlin I estimate only ten days' march.

This reference to Berlin shows the thought underlying the ultimate execution of the campaign, though as yet the Emperor was far from having formulated any precise plan, for he lacked all the data as to his enemy's movements on which to base one. But, all going well, he felt certain that the threat to

---

1. Actually, the South Germans did drink a good deal of wine at their hosts' expense in the Burgundy country, but as compensation for the damage the vineyards suffered during actual fighting, several regiments entered into permanent contracts with the wine-growers to supply their messes after the War was over, and better Burgundy it has never been my good fortune to encounter.

Berlin would compel his adversary to endeavour to interpose, and in that case, marching in his *"batallion carré"* of 200,000 men he had no reason to fear the result.

On September 9, he again wrote to Berthier:

> If I make war upon Prussia, my 'line of operations' will be Strasbourg, Mannheim, Mayence, Würzburg where I have a fortified place; so that my convoys on the fourth day of their march from Mannheim or Mayence can find shelter there. I want also, four days further on, another small place in Bavaria to serve as a depot.

Ultimately Kronach was selected, and Forchheim placed in a state of defence. The line of the Naab was also ordered to be reconnoitred in case of Austrian interference, and reports on Naumburg, Gotha and Leipzig were called for as possible points of support to the advance on Berlin.

On the 10th another letter is dispatched to the Major-General:

> The movements of the Prussians continue to be most extraordinary. They want to get a lesson—my horses leave to-morrow and the Guards in a few days. If the news continues to indicate that the Prussians have lost their heads, I shall go straight to Würzburg, or to Bamberg.

The last phrase, as Bonnal points out (p. 41), shows that the Emperor was still in doubt as to his ultimate direction. If the enemy moved down into the Valley of the Lower Main, then Würzburg became the centre of assembly—if the hesitations of the Prussians continued to afford the opening for the march on Berlin, then Bamberg was best suited to his purpose. On the same day he also ordered his brother Louis (the King of Holland) "to form a camp of 30,000 men at Utrecht to defend Wesel and the north of your dominions."

On September 12 the ambassadors of France at Berlin and Dresden were instructed to inform Berthier immediately if Prussian troops entered Saxony, and on the next day (15th) there followed a most important dispatch to Berthier, shifting the centre of assembly from Würzburg to Bamberg, and detailing the movements to give effect to this diversion, which were to commence the moment news of the violation of Saxon neutrality by Prussian troops should arrive.

Evidently at this date the Emperor still had more than a doubt as to the conduct] of Austria, for neither Soult nor the Bavarian Army (20,000) is as yet withdrawn from observation of the frontier, and this was the probable reason for the renunciation of his offensive design in all its original simplicity—for Würzburg favours an offensive-defensive defence of Southern Germany, against a double danger from North and East, better than Bamberg. If the Prussians marched on Mayence picking up the Hessians as reinforcements on the way, whilst Austria attacked from the east, Napoleon's dilemma at Bamberg would have been a difficult one to solve. Fortunately, however, this condition of doubt did not long remain, for on the 15th, as a consequence presumably of other information which he received, the centre of Assembly, i.e. the position of Army Headquarters and the bulk of his forces, is transferred to Bamberg the moment the news comes in that the Ambassador, Laforest, has quitted Berlin, but not a man is to be moved in anticipation. It is therefore clear that he is still in doubt as to the issue of negotiations, though the Prussians have already been on the move for six weeks.

On September 16 the doubt as to his immediate operations evidently still lingers, for on this day he writes to Berthier, calling attention to the necessity of providing each Division with some 400 to 500 sets of entrenching tools additional to the 1,500 sets already carried by the Corps Headquarters. Bonnal questions whether in this instance Napoleon had not delayed the orders for assembly longer than was wise in view of the information he had already acquired. He knew the positions held by the Prussian troops up to September 7 and 8, and had these immediately proceeded to concentrate either towards Schweinfurt or Coburg-Baireuth, the Grand Army could hardly be drawn together in numbers sufficient to avert the risk of defeat even if the news from the Ambassador had reached Berthier on this very day (16th), or had the latter been thoroughly up to his work.

But this he seldom proved to be, and at this moment he was sending letters to the Emperor which sufficiently disclose his state of mind. Thus on the 17th he wrote detailing all the current rumours in Munich, and almost imploring the Emperor to hasten his coming, reminding him of his letter of February 14, which ordered him to limit himself to the "punctual execution" of orders received. Fortunately his period of suspense was not prolonged, for from the 18th onward the Emperor issued all Army Orders himself, and at 11 p.m. that night the Imperial Guards began their movement in post chaises from Paris for Mayence.[1]

During the 19th and 20th two letters were dispatched to his brother Louis, King of Holland, ordering him to demonstrate with Cavalry from the lower Rhine, and to spread reports in all the papers as to the assembly of an Army of 80,000 men about Wesel. The small Corps which formed the foundation for this rumour was to be set in motion on October 1 and instructed to compensate for its numerical weakness by dispersion and activity.

During the night of September 18-19, news seems to have arrived which set at rest the Emperor's doubts as to the conduct of Austria, for the next morning he dictated to Clarke, his Minister of War, "the general dispositions for the reunion of the Grand Army," the basic document for the whole campaign. According to this instrument the troops were to occupy the following positions.

---

1. For details of this remarkable transport feat see Bonnal, p. 363.

V Corps (Lefebvre)	Koenigshofen	October 3
VII Corps (Augereau)	Assembled around Frankfort	
	Advance Guard Giessen	October 2
IIIrd Corps (Davout)	Bamberg	October 3
IV Corps (Soult)	Amberg	October 4
I Corps (Bernadotte)	Nuremberg	October 2
VI Corps (Ney)	Ansbach	October 2
Park and heavy Staff		
Baggage	Würzburg	October 3
Field Head Quarters	Bamberg	October 3

This order took all day to copy out and was dispatched on the morning of the 20th, reaching Munich on the morning of the 24th.

The men were to carry four days' rations on their persons and ten days' rations were to be conveyed for them in the trains. This amount, unusual in the French Army in those days, being required owing to the inhospitable nature of the districts they might have to traverse, but like many similar orders it seems to have received but partial execution.

A Division of the Bavarian Army, 6,000 strong, was also ordered to report to Bernadotte, but never reached him, as the latter protested emphatically against being burdened with them, and presumably the other Marshals followed suit, for ultimately Napoleon kept them under his own command, but well in rear. They took no part in the fighting and were used to occupy Dresden, where, according to French accounts, they committed all kinds of excesses. On the same day, the creation of a new Corps, the VIII, under Mortier, was ordered, to relieve the VII at Frankfort if the latter were ordered towards Würzburg.

In these positions the Army was still free to adapt itself to the Prussian movements. If the latter moved westwards on the Rhine, the V Corps became the Advance Guard of the whole Army, and, converging with the VII could hold the enemy until the main body had time to arrive. If, on the contrary, he moved through Saxony *via* Hof towards Franconia then

Bernadotte became the Advance Guard, and the V and IV Corps could manoeuvre against his flanks. Hence, though the Emperor undoubtedly had in his mind the movements to be executed in either case, no further instructions were issued until the receipt of more positive information placed the enemy's intentions beyond all doubt.

In the meantime, various instructions modifying the distribution of the Cavalry, organising the Park of Engineers, allocating funds (very insufficiently) for the preparation for defence of sundry old-fashioned fortalices, etc., etc., were sent off to the Army, where they certainly cannot have contributed to correct the state of chaos which Berthier's want of initiative was rapidly developing.

On September 22, the Emperor fixed his departure from Paris for the 25th, and his arrival at Mayence for the 28th. On the same day he ordered the organization of the following roads as "Routes de l'Armée" or lines of communication.

(a) From Mayence to Bamberg, *via* Frankfurt Aschaffenburg, Würzburg.

(b) Augsburg and Ulm to Bamberg, *via* Ellwangen Ansbach and Nürenberg.

The road Mannheim to Würzburg *via* Neckar, Elz and Boxbergh was to be reconnoitred as an alternative, showing that the possibility of a Prussian advance towards the Rhine was still before his mind's eye.

On September 24, Berthier's letters of September 19 and 20 were received by the Emperor. These, as already mentioned, were couched in a despondent tone, and together with repeated rumours, according to which the Prussian concentrations towards Hof and Magdeburg were far more advanced than was really the case, seem somewhat to have upset his balance, as he immediately dictated in reply instructions for Soult to be hurried forward to Amberg by October 1 and to Davout to hasten his concentration on Oettingen, not on Bamberg, the point originally assigned to him. Fortunately

Berthier had left Munich before these instructions reached him, and had gone to Würzburg, where he arrived on the 28th, having taken forty-two hours over the journey of about 160 miles; hence they appear never to have been acted upon, or the trouble in Davout's case might have been serious.

On the same day (28th) the Emperor reached Mayence, and to his surprise found no dispatches from Berthier awaiting him. The delay seems seriously to have affected both his temper and his judgment, for on the morning of the 29th he wrote to the Major-General ordering him to instruct Bernadotte to march on Kronach and then take up with his command, "a good position protecting the passage into Saxony," but not to cross the frontier. The evident intention being to force the hands of the Prussians in Saxony and prevent them from the westward movement, which (though he was quite prepared to deal with it), would nevertheless have thrown the focus of the fighting into a difficult country where great decisions were not easily attainable.

The V Corps was again reminded to send out spies and secret reconnaissances towards Fulda, for if Berthier's information of the 20th proved correct, it would be too late to carry out the proposed invasion of Saxony.

Other instructions then follow, dealing with the Cavalry, which show *that the Emperor had completely forgotten his previous orders on the same subject, and that no one was at hand to remind him of them*.

In his second letter he corrects his mistake of the 24th, in ordering Davout to Oettingen, admitting that he should have written Bamberg, but such a confession is indeed rare in his writings, and goes far to explain the unreadiness of his subordinates to accept responsibility, which unreadiness grew steadily more pronounced as time went on. It must always be borne in mind in criticising them, that Napoleon never took any of his Marshals into his confidence until the very last instant, *so that throughout all the anxious moments of these great re-*

unions, all were working in the dark, generally in profound ignorance of the orders received by their immediate neighbours. When a battle was actually in sight, he wrote fully and clearly to all concerned, as we shall presently see, but there can be no doubt that his movements to that end might have been greatly facilitated had he only trusted his subordinates more entirely.

Having sent off these two letters to Berthier, he now sent for Murat, who being related to the Imperial family he trusted more implicitly, and after verbal instructions (which have not been preserved) he gave him the interim command of the Army, over Berthier's head, and sent him off to Würzburg with the following written instructions to guide him:

> It is to Würzburg, not Bamberg, that Prince Murat is to proceed, because Würzburg will serve equally well as the point of departure for operations against Fulda, or Erfurt, or Leipzig.[1]

Whether this interim appointment was intended to relieve Berthier of the enormous burden of work which his position entailed, or because he was not at hand to receive verbal instructions, (the Emperor apparently having forgotten that he had cancelled his order to him to come to Mayence,) does not appear, but it seems that his supersession was never communicated to Berthier, who continued to send orders direct to the Marshals, so that until the Emperor personally took over the- command of the whole Army on October 3, a dual command existed which led to some confusion and much friction.

Hardly had this letter to Murat been dispatched (it is dated September 29, 10 a.m.), than Berthier's belated courier arrived, closely followed by the reports of two spies which completely changed the Emperor's appreciation of the situation. Instead of the Prussians being in the advanced positions indicated by Berthier's alarmist letters of the 20th (see above), it was now

---

1. Bonnal, p. 118.

clear that as late as September 27 they were still about Eisenach, Meiningen and Hildburghausen, and the Saxons could not be more than a couple of marches south of Dresden. Hence there would be ample time for the Grand Army to cross the defiles of the mountains and the Saale, and deploy beyond them before serious interference could be expected.

The Emperor now sat down to work *and achieved one of the records of his life.* He had been travelling and working night and day since he left Paris on the 26th, had then spent thirty-six hours of anxious expectation at Mayence, and now he began to write and dictate almost uninterruptedly till the early morning hours of October 2, snatching only a couple of hours' sleep as opportunity afforded. His letters of the first twenty-four hours contain some of his clearest reasoning, but by degrees his mind tires, and many of the latter ones contain quite incoherent ideas, giving evidence of extreme mental fatigue.

What the state of the unfortunate Major-General must have been, as this avalanche of instructions tumbled in upon him, it is indeed difficult to conceive, for he was still in the dark as to the meaning of the many changes introduced. At any rate, the orders did not become more lucid as they filtered through his brain, and as Murat was also issuing orders at the same time, the confusion in the Army became extreme.

It is in the letters of the 29th, four in number, sent by special messenger to the King of Holland, that the whole of Napoleon's design is first revealed. For dynastic reasons it was communicated to him alone, the Marshals receiving only the merest indications of their probable parts in the coming drama. In his first note, Napoleon begins by stating—

> It is my intention to concentrate *all my forces* on my right, leaving the space between the Rhine and Bamberg entirely open, so as to be able to unite about 200,000 men on the same field of battle.

If the enemy pushes parties between Mayence and Bamberg, I shall not let that disturb me, because my line of communications will be by Forchheim, and from thence by Würzburg.

The nature of the events which may take place is incalculable, because the enemy who supposes my left to be on the Rhine and my right on Bohemia, and believes that my line of operations is parallel to my battle-front, may see great advantage in turning my left, and in that case I can throw him into the Rhine.

October 10 to 14, the VIII Corps will arrive at Mayence, about 18,000-20,000 strong. Its instructions will be to make incursions as far as Frankfort, but not to allow itself to be cut off from the Rhine, in case of necessity retiring behind it, and seeking communication with your troops.

His second letter begins:

The observations in my first note are all of a precautionary nature.

My first marches menace the heart of the Prussian Monarchy, and the deployment of my forces will be so imposing and rapid, that it is probable that the whole Army of Westphalia will retire on Magdeburg, and all will combine by forced marches for the defence of the capital.

Then, but only then, it will be necessary for you to throw out an advance guard to take possession of the Mark, Münster, Osnabrück and East Frisia, *by small mobile columns, radiating from a central point.*

For the first part of the War you are only a corps of observation—i.e. until the enemy has been thrown into the Elbe—I only count on your corps as a means of diversion to amuse the enemy up to October 12, which is the date on which my plans will be unmasked. Finally, in case of a serious event, such as the loss of a great battle, whilst I make good my retreat to the Danube, you can defend Wesel and Mayence with your Army and the VIII Corps, which latter is under no circumstances to be withdrawn from Mayence.

In the third and fourth letters, Napoleon develops the previous ideas, and adds instructions for his brother after his (Napoleon's) first successful battle to enter Cassel, disarm the troops and drive out the Elector. Meanwhile, however, he is to be most careful not to excite the latter's suspicions or to induce his hostility. His neutrality is always worth preserving as it may keep 10,000 to 12,000 troops away from the battlefield, Finally, he concludes with this remarkable passage—

> The least check to you will cause me anxiety; my measures may thereby be disconcerted, and such an event might leave the whole of the north of my Empire without a head. On the other hand, whatever may happen to me, as long as I know you are behind the Rhine, I can act with greater freedom; even if some great misfortune overtakes me, I shall beat my enemies if I have only 50,000 men left, because free to manoeuvre, independent of all lines of operations and tranquil as to the most important points of my Empire, I shall always have resources and means.

As the net result of all this writing the VII Corps (Augereau) was moved up to Würzburg, and one way or another in spite of the conflicting orders from the Emperor, Berthier and Murat the whole Army reached on October 3 their positions, which practically differ little from those originally indicated in his first order for the "Reunion" of the Army of September 19th, and one is tempted to wonder whether it would not have been better for all concerned had Napoleon done a little more writing from February 14th to September, and considerably less from September 19th to October 1st. If Berthier and the Marshals were good enough to work their commands for all the months before September, they were fit to be entrusted with the general outline of the Emperor's plans, and in this case *the whole of the necessary marching orders could very reasonably have been dictated within three hours at the very outside!*[1]

It is not so much that the Emperor overworked himself, on the contrary, his physical health was never better as he wrote to the Empress detailing his day's work, "it agreed with him and he was putting on weight daily," but the consequences to his harassed Staff were most calamitous, for it would seem that it was now that there first crept into the French Staff the habit of deliberately framing orders capable of being interpreted in several ways, which practice proved so disastrous in 1870 (*vide* Bonnal's *Manoeuvre de St. Privat*). In order to cover their own responsibility orders were framed admitting of two or more interpretations. If the recipient chose the right one, the Staff congratulated itself on its perspicacity, if, on the other hand, events proved the recipient wrong in his action, they pointed to the order and said, "Why, of course that was not what the order meant, any fool could have seen that!" [2]

---

1. This reunion of the Army called for tremendous marching from many of the units; thus the VII Corps marched 25, 20, 24 miles on three consecutive days; the 2nd Division of the corps even 30 miles on the last day, and Legendre's Brigade (22nd and 96th) covered 25, 24, 21, 30, 30, 25, 25, 20, 20 in nine consecutive days, an average of 24 miles a day, the last three days through a mountainous country. *See* Bonnal, p. 172 and 189.
2. A typical error may be cited in support from the 1870 Campaign. Where two alternative roads led to the same destination from a given point—thus, one being safe, the other doubtful. To cover their responsibility the Staff would order the troops to March from A via B to C, leaving it to the Commanding Officer to make his choice. Of course the order should have run from A via E (or D) to C.

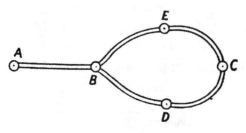

Want of space compels one to limit the extracts from this forty-eight hours' output of Napoleon's energy, I can only cite one more instance of the confusion of thought originating from too-long concentration of effort, but those who are interested in the question should peruse the whole correspondence given by Foucart. Thus in his letter to Berthier, October 1, 2 a.m., these passages follow each other in sequence—

> The depots of the Cavalry are to be united at Forcheim. We must count on the enemy coming to Würzburg.
>
> I am asking 600 men from the Elector of Hesse.
>
> All the convalescents of the Army, about 12 to 15 per regiment are to be sent to ——.[1]

All these items had to be extracted from their place in the text and made the subject of a special letter to the departments concerned, and as these are not isolated instances, one can imagine the constant strain on the attention of the recipient to see that no single pearl of strategical indication, such as the allusion to Würzburg, should escape amongst the mass of irrelevant detail.

During the course of October 2 the Emperor moved on to Würzburg, where he remained until the 6th. Here he received the numerous Engineer Officers (who had been despatched to reconnoitre the roads into Saxony) and cross-examined them at considerable length. The spies also reported direct to him, and the picture he was finally able to evolve of his enemies' positions differed but very little from the actual facts, though it conveyed no indication of their probable movements. October 4 was a day of relative rest for him, as all the troops were not yet in position, and except two orders, one to Marshal Lefebvre (V Corps), the other to Marshal Augereau (VII Corps) directing them to take the road towards Coburg, drafted by Berthier, but presumably inspired by him, no other letters for this day have been traced.

---

1. *See* Bonnal, p. 176, and Foucart.

On the 5th the general order for the passage of the Frank-enwald by the Grand Army was prepared by Berthier, and the Emperor wrote seven letters, three of great importance, to the Major-General, to Soult, and to Bernadotte.

In the first he directs especial attention to the defences of Würzburg, as the movement of the V Corps towards Coburg would leave it exposed to attack, and actually at that very moment a small command of Prussian Hussars under Müffling was on its way to attempt a surprise. Doubtless it would have achieved a considerable measure of success but for this timely warning, for it was as difficult in the Grand Army, as in any other, to spare men of first-rate ability and energy for commands on the lines of communications.

The next letter to Soult is one of the best known from the Emperor's pen, and deserves the closest study, for it gives the most complete revelation of Napoleon's idea of the *"bataillon carre"* form of manoeuvre, as it presented itself to its inventor, that has been handed down to us.

> I think it advisable that you should know my plans so that you may have a guide to your action in important circumstances.
>
> I have caused Würzburg, Forchheim and Kronach to be armed and provisioned, and I propose to debouch into Saxony with my whole Army in three columns. You are at the head of the right column with the Corps of Marshal Ney half a day's march behind you, and 10,000 Bavarians another day's march behind him, which makes in all over 50,000 men.
>
> Marshal Bernadotte leads the centre column, behind him follows Davout's Corps, the greater part of the Reserve Cavalry and my Guards, which gives about 70,000 men.
>
> He marches by Kronach, Lobenstein, and Schleiz.
>
> The V Corps is at the head of the left column, followed

by the VII, and the two march by Coburg, Grafenthal, and Saalfeld. This makes another 40,000 men.

The day you arrive at Hof, the whole will have reached positions on the same alignment.

I shall march with the centre.

With this immense superiority of force united in a space so narrow, you will feel that I am determined to leave nothing to chance, and can attack the enemy wherever he chooses to stand with nearly double his numbers.

It appears that the arm from which we have most to fear in the Prussian Army, is their Cavalry; but with such Infantry as you command, and being always ready to form squares, you have little to trouble about. Since, however, in war no means should ever be neglected, take care to have from 3,000 to 5,000 sets of entrenching tools with your Divisions, so as to be able to make, if necessary, a redoubt or a simple trench.

If the enemy does not show forces against you exceeding 30,000 men, you can concert with Marshal Ney and attack him, but if he is in a position he has held for long, he will have reconnoitred and entrenched himself. In that case, be prudent!

On reaching Hof, your first care should be to open communications between Lobenstein, Ebersdorf and Schleiz; on that day (October 10), I shall be at Ebersdorf.

From the news which has come in up to to-day it appears that if the enemy makes any movement, it will be against my left, as the bulk of his forces seem to be about Erfurt.

I cannot recommend you too earnestly to correspond with me frequently, and keep me fully informed of all you learn from the direction of Dresden

Vous pensez bien que ce serait une belle affaire que de se porter autour de cette place (Dresden) *en un bataillon carre de 200,000 hommes. Cependant tout cela demande un peu d'art et quelques evenements.*

I give this last phrase in the original, *because it may be considered to form the very foundation-stone of the whole of the modern "doctrine" of the French Staff.* It is so casually introduced and so loosely worded that though it has been quoted again and again in all Napoleonic studies, its full importance was never formulated until some ninety years afterwards, when, taken in conjunction with the Emperor's demands made upon the *"avant garde generale," viz.,* not merely *to observe and report,* but *to attack and fix*[1] the enemy, it suddenly dawned on men's minds that it was in the sense of security which this *"bataillon carre"* conception conveyed, that the real secret of Napoleon's strategic success was to be found.

After all, in itself it was no new idea, even the Crusaders had instinctively adapted it to fight their way through hordes of light-armed and mobile antagonists.

Moreover, in India, only three years before, Lord Lake had been employing it, even more literally, to force a path through the swarming Light Horse of the Mahrattas, but the idea had dropped out of contemporary European strategy, as a consequence of the growth of the Magazine system, and the resultant increase in susceptibility of the communications.

In the remaining correspondence of the day, the Emperor arranges the order of departure of the several heads of columns on the basis of the last news available. The Prussian Main body being still about Erfurt, the left column is the most exposed, and hence to avert any possible hindrance to its exit from the mountains, the right-hand column (Soult) is given a day's start, so as to be able to sweep down from the east and outflank any possible concentration which the enemy might attempt against either the centre or left columns. But this alteration, though it mars the symmetry of the design, detracts nothing from the general principle. Meanwhile, all the columns close up within

---

1. *"On ne manoeuvre pas qu'autour d'un point fixe."*

themselves (there had been considerable lengthening out, owing to the great heat, and the bad qualities of the roads), and the Infantry are assembled in masses, as far as the nature of the ground allows, to flood the enemy's country on a broad front the moment the final order to advance is issued. The Cavalry is held back until all the passages through the mountains and over the Saale are clear.

On October 5, also, Lannes was ordered to take over the command of the V Corps. Lefebvre had not given proofs of much capacity during the month he had been at its head, and the Emperor doubtless felt that he was unequal to the demands which this, the most dangerous post in the whole Army, might make upon him. The opening phrase of the Order of Supersession is too useful a model to be lost. "The Emperor desiring to employ you more particularly about his person, etc., appoints you to the command of a Division of his Guard."

War had not as yet been declared, but the Emperor was not the man to allow the observance of any such formality to endanger the possibility, now within his reach, of effecting his deployment beyond the mountains to escape him, and all being in readiness, orders were issued during the course of October 6 for the columns of the left and centre to commence their movement next day. No less than sixteen such orders were required by Berthier, though as Bonnal points out (p. 336), four would have abundantly sufficed. But in spite of this excess of energy on his part, they were so badly drafted that much friction ensued, and indeed Augereau was kept waiting for forty-eight hours at Coburg. Thus Lannes, in the post of danger, was left single-handed to face a possible offensive of the Prussians, and actually found himself compelled to attack Prince Louis at Saalfeld, in spite of the formal recommendation of the Emperor not to engage the enemy without being assured of adequate support.

Fortunately, the information that the whole of Prince Hohenlohe's Army was in the vicinity of Saalfeld and Neustadt, which led the Emperor to impose such caution upon Lannes, proved incorrect. As already mentioned in the previous chapter, Prince Louis' command was quite inadequate to check a whole French Corps d'Armee and with the exception of this contretemps, and a trifling engagement with some advanced parties of Tauenzein's, Division at Saalburg on October 8, and at Schleiz, the whole passage of the mountains was effected without incident, and on the evening of October 11, the Grand Army was deployed on the Saxon plains ready for the next stage of the campaign.

That night the troops and the Headquarters of the several Corps occupied the following positions; the troops themselves bivouacking along the roads, practically in order of march, and resuming their movement next day by units, without wasting time by forming up in brigades or divisions, *viz.*: V Corps, Neustadt; VII Corps, Saalfeld; I Corps, Gera—Cavalry in advance as far as Crossen on the Elster; III Corps, Mittel Pöllnitz, Guard, Auma; IV Corps, Weyda; VI Corps, Schleiz.

The Emperor, however, was not without perplexities, for the conduct of the enemy had been so erratic that he found it difficult to form a true conception of his actual movements. Moreover, until late on the night of October 11-12, he did not know the whereabouts of Marshal Lannes. He had expected to find the Prussian Army concentrated at Gera, but only stragglers had been found there, and Murat's reports pointed to Roda as the place on which the troops, beaten at Saalfeld and Schleiz had retired. Roda might, therefore, well be the point of reunion of Hohenlohe's Army, and in that case the main Prussian Army must clearly intend to cross to the right bank of the Saale from Kahla and Lobeda, and the battle he so earnestly desired was close at hand.

With this idea in his mind he had already dispatched orders for the I Corps to remain at Gera, as an advanced echelon of the right wing, with the IV towards Ebersdorf in support. The III was to be at Mittel Pöllnitz as centre, the VI at Neustadt on the left, and the V and VII in echelon between Saalfeld and Neustadt in support of the left.[1] Then between 1 and 2 a.m. of the 12th definite news arrived which completely upset the plans he had formed and led to the combination out of which the manoeuvre of Jena finally resulted.

This fateful information arose from the capture of a Saxon convoy near Gera by Lasalle. Lasalle did not send off his report of the event until 8 p.m. to Murat (his superior officer) at Gera, and the latter did not transmit it to the Emperor till 11 p.m. The report contained the words, "The prisoners say that the King is at Erfurt with 200,000 men," which Murat amplified into, "The latest information I have been able to procure seems to confirm what your Majesty has already received relative to the concentration of the enemy about Erfurt."[2] On receipt of this communication Napoleon set himself down to think hard, and two hours later the idea of the manoeuvre of Jena had taken final shape in his brain.

This is how Bonnal describes its evolution. Having believed on the strength of a report sent in by Soult on the 9th, 8 p.m. (which turned out to be incorrect) that the Prussians were concentrating on Gera, the Emperor had persuaded himself that Prince Hohenlohe at Roda formed the advance Guard of the Prussian forces united between Jena and Weimar.

The report from Murat just received, destroyed this presumption, and suggested that the Prussians were falling back on Erfurt. In that case Hohenlohe was only calling in his detachments and was retiring on Jena.

It was not possible to suppose that the Prussians meant to fight with their backs against the Harz Mountains. Hence the presumption was that they intended to fall back behind the Elbe, and they had only three roads available for the purpose—

---

1. Bonnal, p. 398.
2. Bonnal, p. 399.

(a) by Gotha, Nordhausen and Halberstadt on Magdeburg.

(b) to Magdeburg by Eisleben.

(c) Weimar, by Kösen, Freiburg, Halle on Dessau, and Napoleon was aware of the presence of the Duke of Würtemberg's "strategic reserve" between Halle and Dessau, 15,000 strong.

They might use any or all of these three roads, and the simplest way of preventing their doing so was to direct a strong force (I Corps and Cavalry) towards Dessau to destroy the strategic reserve and gain a footing on the right bank of the Elbe, thus compromising the further defence of that river, and to send another column (the III Corps) to Naumburg, as rapidly as possible, from whence to strike at the Eisleben road and hold the enemy upon it until the main Army crossing the Saale at Kahla and Lobeda could overtake him.

In case the Prussians stood fast at Erfurt and Weimar, then the movement of the I and III Corps must not be too wide to prevent their arrival in time to take part in the decisive battle.

With this general picture of affairs in his mind, he drafted out a rough note for a concentration for a battle, to be fought about Weimar on the 16th, which has, fortunately, been rediscovered in the French Archives, and runs as follows—

Guard (Cavalry) 10th evening at Bamberg, 11th at Lichterfels, 12th Kronach, 13th at Lobenstein.

D'Hautpoul (1st Division of Cuirassiers), 11th, two leagues in front of Kronach, 14th, at Auma, 15th, at Jena.

Klein (1st Division of Dragoons), 11th, two leagues in front of Kronach, 15th, at Jena, 14th, Jena, 15th, at Auma. Klein, on the 12th, to Lobenstein.

Jena to Weimar, 4 leagues; Naumburg to Weimar, 7 leagues; Kahla to Weimar, 5 leagues; Neustadt to Jena, 5 leagues; Gera to Jena, 7 leagues; Zeitz to Jena, 7 leagues; Reserve Cavalry, 14th, at Jena; Guards, 15th, to Jena; Park, 15th, to Auma; Davout 14th, to Apolda; Lannes, 15th, to Weimar; Augereau, 14th, at Mellingen; Bernadotte, the 14th, to Dornburg; Soult, 14th, to Jena; Ney, 14th, to Kahla.

He then wrote to Lannes the following most characteristic letter—

> Auma, 4 a.m.
> October 12th

All the intercepted letters show that the enemy has lost his head. They hold counsels day and night and do not know what steps to take next.

You will see by the orders of the Major-General which follow, that I bar the roads from Dresden and from Berlin against them.

The Art to-day is to attack the enemy wherever you meet him and beat him in detail whilst in the act of concentrating.

When I say, 'attack everything you meet,' I mean everything on the march, not what is in position.

The Prussians have already sent one column on Frankfurt (Rüchel) which they had soon to withdraw. So far they have displayed their thorough ignorance of the Art of War.

Do not forget to send out many scouts, to intercept the mails, travellers, etc., and collect as much information as possible.

If the enemy moves from Erfurt on Saalfeld, which would be absurd (but in his position one may expect all sorts of happenings), you will unite with Marshal Augereau and fall on his flank.

The order from the Major-General alluded to above was couched in the following form—

To Marshal Lannes at Neustadt

4.30 a.m.

Will move on Jena by Kahla. Marshal Augereau is ordered to Kahla. The intention of the Emperor is that as soon as you arrive at Jena you should take all possible steps to find out what the enemy has been doing during the last three days.

It will be noticed that neither letter nor order conveys a useful hint to guide its recipient, or inform him what the scope of the immediate manoeuvre is really intended to be, and the opening assertion "all the intercepted letters," etc., clashes acutely with the concluding paragraph of the order, *viz.*, to "find out what the enemy has been doing for the last three days."

The statement about barring the roads to Dresden and Berlin is decidedly premature, as in fact the latter via Freiburg—Merseburg, and Dessau was not even closed on the morning of the 14th, and the elementary instructions in scouting duties would seem more in place in a communication to a humble patrol leader than in a letter to the finest Advance Guard Commander of his epoch. Nor are his letters to the other Marshals, Murat and Soult, more helpful. Not one receives even an indication of the plan in their master's mind. *Imagine the consequences had a stray Prussian bullet removed him during the course of the next forty-eight hours!*

The net result of all the orders dispatched as a consequence of the receipt of Murat's belated dispatch was that Murat marched to Naumburg next morning scouting over the whole plain towards Leipzig and Wessenfels.

Bernadotte followed Murat, and reached the line Meinweh-Zeitz.

Davout reached Naumburg. Soult, Gera. Ney, Mittel Pöllnitz. Lannes, Burgau. Augereau, Kahla.[1]

1. The columns of Lannes and Augereau were already well on their way when the second orders overtook them and obliged them to counter-march. Hence they did not reach the Saale till late in the afternoon.

The two latter, it will be observed, were on the left bank of the Saale within twelve to fourteen miles of Weimar, Where the enemy was supposed to be, and about half that distance from Capellendorf and Isserstedt, where he actually was. The country to their left was broken and intersected, and only the weak Cavalry force, which had been left to the Corps on the reorganisation of September 29, was available for scouting.

Whilst these orders were on their way the Emperor wrote another letter to Talleyrand which deserves quoting.

Affairs are moving here as I calculated two months ago (i.e. August 12) in Paris, march by march, event by event, I have not been deceived in a single point. There will be some interesting happenings within the next two or three days; but all appears to confirm me in the opinion that the Prussians have no chance of success. Their Generals are 'des grands imbeciles'.

Just before leaving Auma for Gera, he wrote to Davout apparently as an after-thought, the one gleam of true inspiration he had received during this notable twelve hours.

It is possible that the enemy may execute his movement of retreat between the Ilm and the Saale, for it seems to me he is evacuating Jena. It will be easy for you to ascertain this on your arrival at Naumburg.

As it happened this was the precise movement the Prussians were deciding to carry out, and how near it came to success will be apparent hereafter.

October 13th. On reaching Gera, Napoleon, according to his usual custom in the field, turned in for a few hours rest at 8 p.m., rising again at midnight to receive the reports from the front, and issue the necessary orders. *This was perhaps the principal secret of the extraordinary mobility developed by French troops under his personal command.* He brought his mind fresh to his task, and with the latest possible information before him, he was able to issue orders which would require no alteration except in extreme cases. This work finished by about 2 a.m., he wrote explanatory letters, whilst Berthier and the Staff prepared the orders for dispatch, and the bearers were generally away with their dispatches in time to reach the farthest troops while these were still cooking their morning meal. In most armies of the period, and indeed for many years afterwards, it was the custom to issue orders during the afternoon, then to adjourn for supper, and if, as frequently happened, the day's reports necessitated alterations, no one brought, let us say an unjaded mind, to bear on the subject. *Hence the invariable sequence "ordre, contreordre, désordre."*

This night it happened that up to 3 a.m. no fresh news had been received from either of the three columns and only some artillery fire had been heard from the direction of Lannes, due that afternoon at Lobeda. Hence the orders transmitted were mostly administrative, and only Ney was instructed to march from Auma to Roda and let the men clean up their arms. Murat was warned that the whole Army was to have a day's rest, to fill up ammunition wagons, procure provisions, and collect stragglers.

7 a.m. When up to 7 a.m. no reports from Lannes, Davout, or Murat had been received, the Emperor grew impatient and sent off three officers, one to each column, to collect information, and bring him a personal report. They were to inform the Marshal that the Emperor would be at Jena at 1 p.m., passing by way of Roda. In his note to Murat he says: "My intention is to march straight for the enemy. If he is at Erfurt, I shall move on Weimar and attack him on the 16th," which is proof of the hold his design of the night of the 12th had acquired over his mind.

9 a.m. Shortly after the departure of these three officers, the belated reports arrived.

Augereau wrote from Kahla:

The enemy was at Jena, but I am assured that he has left, and is moving on Weimar. It is said that from Weimar he will retire on Erfurt, where the main body under the King is gathered.

Davout from Naumburg, 10 p.m. October 12, after reporting the incidents of the march sums up the situation as follows:

All the reports of deserters, prisoners and inhabitants unite in placing the Prussian Army at Erfurt, Weimar, and that neighbourhood. It is certain that the King arrived yesterday (11th) at Weimar. No enemy between Leipzig and Naumburg.

Finally from Zeitz, late on the evening of the 12th, Murat forwards the report of a secret agent, who had traversed the whole line of march of the Prussians from Fulda (reaching Erfurt on the 7th, Naumburg on the 8th), and found troops all along his route. The King and Queen were at Erfurt.

All three seem specially intended to confirm him in his preconception, and at once he sat down and wrote to Murat, the well-known letter beginning *"Enfin, le voile est déchiré,"* and continuing:

The enemy commences his retreat on Magdeburg, move as quickly as possible with Bernadotte's Corps on Dornburg. Above all, bring your Dragoons and Light Cavalry. I believe the enemy will either attack Lannes at Jena or endeavour to evade him. In the former case your position at Dornburg will enable you to assist him.

An orderly officer was also at once despatched towards Auma to intercept the Reserve Cavalry and switch it on to the Roda-Jena road, and Soult, who was on the spot, was directed to the same place, his troops to march all night if necessary.

10 a.m. These arrangements having been made, the Emperor then composed the celebrated fourth Bulletin of the Grand Army to announce the coming annihilation of the Prussians.

The Prussian Army is caught *'en flagrant delit,'* it is turned, the anniversary of the affairs round Ulm (October 15, 1805) will be celebrated in the history of France.

No more confident prophecy was ever based on such very slender grounds, for as we shall presently see, during the next twenty-four hours the fate of Napoleon and his Army more than once skirted the abyss of disaster.

Napoleon then mounted and rode towards Jena, passing through Langenburg and Kostritz.

3 p.m. About 3 p.m., being then about four miles from Jena, a report despatched by Lannes dated noon was handed to him, and the sound of heavy musketry fire came over to him from the same direction.

Lannes reported the presence of an enemy's Corps of some 12 to 15,000 men above the town, and according to the reports current among the inhabitants, the King still in Erfurt on the 11th, and 20,000 to 25,000 men between Jena and Weimar. Reconnaissances are being sent out to determine the latter point. The report ends up:

> I desire to know whether it is the intention of your Majesty that I should march my Corps upon Weimar. *I dare not assume the responsibility* of ordering this movement for fear your Majesty may have some other destination for me.

It was this well-reasoned appreciation of his duties as Commander of an Advance Guard which to my mind saved the situation. Had Lannes gone for his enemy in the bull-at-a-gate fashion of the Prussian Corps Commanders at Spicheren, Woerth and Verneville in 1870, Massenbach's fatal message would have arrived too late, and Napoleon's Grand Army (at least that section of it under his personal command) would never have found room to accomplish their deployment beyond the Saale. Now Lannes was the one man amongst all others who feared the Emperor's anger least, and this mixture of cool caution with his well-known daring as a leader of troops, seems never to have attracted all the attention it deserves. *This is the ideal standard of conduct for an independent subordinate.*

Returning now to Napoleon,—having read this report he dictated from the saddle four immediate orders. Marshal Lefebvre to march the Guard to Jena; (2) Soult to hasten his march on Jena; (3) Ney to push as far as possible towards Jena; (4) Davout to manoeuvre against the enemy's left, this same evening, if he heard artillery fire from Jena—if not to wait orders for the morrow.

4.30 p.m. Shortly after 4 p.m. the Emperor rode up the slopes of the Landgrafenberg, where he met Lannes. From thence he could only see the outposts of Tauenzien's Division, guarding the slopes of the Dornburg and possibly some Saxon tents between, or over, the tops of the Isserstedter copses.[1]

Then under Napoleon's personal superintendence, as soon as it grew dark, the V Corps was brought up to the Plateau of the Landgrafenberg and formed in several lines—Divisions side by side. The Guard as it arrived formed in "mass" behind,

---

1. I lay especial stress on this point, because in all previous accounts of the campaign from the French side that I have hitherto studied, it is invariably asserted that from the summit of the Landgrafenberg, Napoleon could see the camps of several thousand men; some even stating that he could see the main Prussian Army on the march towards Auerstadt. My own recollection of the ground is that his view was distinctly limited by the watershed of the ridge running from the Dornburg towards the Isserstedter Forest, and to make sure I stood upon the Napoleonstein itself to bring my eye to the same level as that of the Emperor when mounted. Possibly the trees in the forest may have been thinner and lower then than when I saw them, though they have probably been cut down twice at least in the interval. But I cannot bring myself to believe either from memory of the ground, or from a study of the map that either he or Lannes at any time saw with their own eyes even a quarter of the strength of the Prussians behind the hill. The story owes its origin, I believe, to Jomini, whose picturesque and facile pen often led him into "terminological inexactitudes," and from Jomini it passed over into Hamley and thence into all accepted British textbooks, thereby perpetuating an entirely false conception of the situation. Bonnal is the only French authority to my knowledge who makes no allusion to this supposed vision into futurity, which has even made its way in a slightly modified form into the history of the battle published last year by the *Revue d'Histoire,* the official organ of the Historical Section of the French General Staff.

and the track up the hillside was improved to enable the guns to get up to the top. Only one fire was lighted on the summit, and by its light the Emperor wrote the following order for the seizure of the ground necessary for further deployment:

> Marshal Augereau commands the left; he will place his first Division in column on the road to Weimar as far as the point at which General Gazan sent his artillery up the hill.[1]
>
> He will keep the necessary forces on the plateau to the left, level with the head of his column, and send out skirmishers all along the enemy's front at different *"debouches des montagnes."* When General Gazan advances, he will follow on to the plateau with his whole Corps, and then march according to circumstances to take the left of the Army.
>
> Marshal Lannes will have at daybreak all his Artillery in his intervals and in the order of battle in which he has passed the night.[2]
>
> The Artillery of the Imperial Guard will be placed on the height[3] and the Guard will be behind the plateau, ranged in five lines, the first line containing the Chasseurs crowning the plateau.
>
> The village, which is on our right[4] will be cannonaded by all General Suchet's artillery,[5] and immediately afterwards stormed and carried.
>
> The Emperor will give the signal. All are to be ready at daybreak.
>
> Marshal Ney will be ready at daybreak, at the extremity of the plateau,[6] to mount and *move on the right* of Mar-

---

1. Gazan's was the left Division of the V Corps.
2. *Divisions side by side, each in three lines.*
3. Landgrafenberg.
4. Closwitz.
5. Should read, "By all the artillery of General Suchet's Division."
6. At the foot of the slopes of the left bank to the north, near Jena.

shal Lannes the moment the village is. taken, and thus room is obtained for deployment.

Marshal Soult will debouch by the road which has been reconnoitred on the right[3] and will manoeuvre as the right of the Army.

The general idea of the battle will be for the Marshals to form in two lines, not counting that of the Light Infantry, at about 300 yards distance. The light Cavalry of each Corps will be placed so as to be at the disposal of each General to employ as circumstances dictate.

The Heavy Cavalry, as soon as it arrives, will be placed on the plateau in reserve behind the Guard, to move as circumstances require.

What is of importance today is to deploy on the plain; dispositions will then be made as the manoeuvres and the force shown by the enemy indicate, to drive him from the positions which he occupies, and which are necessary for our deployment.

Even when every conceivable allowance has been made for the fact that this order was written in semi-darkness—hence the omission of all names of villages, etc.— and though intended only for men on the ground, these orders can hardly serve as a model for our imitation, and had disaster ensued it would not have been difficult for each Marshal to take shelter behind their general vagueness. But though practically none of them in the end received literal execution, owing to the fog, the spirit nevertheless is clear enough, and in fact proved sufficient for the war-trained leaders to whom they were addressed. No reference whatever is made to either the I or III Corps, but these were attended to under separate covers, which, however, contained no reference to the battle, which actually did occur, for the reason that Napoleon was still convinced that no decisive battle was as yet in sight,

---

1. From Lobstedt and Zweten on Rödingen.

and he only brought up the four Corps mentioned and the Guards in order to have men enough at hand to clear the space necessary for his future deployment.

Actually, however, the demands made on the men proved in excess of the marching powers of many. When daylight broke only Lannes, Augereau and the Guards, less the Heavy Cavalry, were in hand. Ney's advance guard only had reached Jena. It lay at the foot of the hill, and St. Hilaire's Division of Soult's Corps was hidden away in the Rauthal out of sight in the fog and completely beyond the Emperor's control. The bulk of the IV Corps being still some miles to the rear. Up to midday on the 14th not more than 42,000 men had reached the field.

NOTE ON AUDIBILITY OF ARTILLERY FIRE.—It will be noted that Davout is ordered to move only if he *heard* artillery fire. It is extraordinary that in the Napoleonic days no one had noticed that though guns may sometimes be heard up to sixty miles and more, on others they cannot be heard at two miles even though clearly visible. The phenomenon was first investigated by Professor Tyndall about 1874, who found that the conductivity of air to sound depended on the uniformity of the tension of aqueous vapour between any two points. Thus under a clear sky and over hard open ground or sea, the reports will travel indefinitely. I myself have heard guns in India at a distance of ninety miles, but if the continuity of aqueous tension is broken—either by the shadow of a passing cloud or by the presence of a sheet of water or mud between two points—the sound is suddenly arrested. Thus from the Isle of Grain the guns at Shoeburyness are distinctly audible at high water, but at half-tide when the Nore sand becomes dry, the sound suddenly ceases though the discharges of the guns are still clearly visible. It should be a standing order that troops once set in motion to the sound of the guns should continue in movement until the Commanding Officer has convinced himself by his own eyes that they have ceased firing. Troops should never halt because the sound of the guns ceases; for illustrations of the danger of doing so, see my *Evolution of Infantry Tactics*.

Marches of the Grand Army During the Passage of the Franconian Forest to the Battle of Jena

V Corps (Lannes)	October 9, 30 miles; 10th, 13 miles, with engagement at Saalfeld; 11th, 20 miles; 12th, 16 miles, engagement at Winzerle; 13th, 4 miles, engagement on Landgrafenberg
VII Corps (Augereau)	Left Coburg 4 p.m., October 10, marched 43 miles and reached Saalfeld in the night of the 11th–12th, about midnight; 12th, Kahla, 24 miles (via Pössneck); 13th, 9 miles
I Corps	October 9, 16 miles, engagement at Schleiz; 10th, 12 miles; 11th, 16 miles (1st Division, 30 miles); 12th, 18 miles; 13th, 10 miles
III Corps (Davout)	October 9, 20 miles; 10th, 14 miles; 11th, 14 miles; 12th (1st Division), 30 miles, (2nd Division) 24 miles; 3rd Division, 17 miles; 13th, 2nd Division, 8 miles; 3rd Division, 14 miles
IV Corps (Soult).	October 8, 18 miles; 9th, 21 miles; 10th, 8 miles; 11th, 18 to 26, according to Divisions; 12th, 10 to 16 miles; 13th, 1st Division, 27 miles; 2nd and 3rd Division, 13 miles
IV Corps (Ney).	October 9, 17 miles; 10th, 26 miles; 11th, 8 to 12 miles; 12th, 10 miles; 13th, 14 miles

Except Augereau's Corps, none were therefore overworked, as generally supposed. I have attended manoeuvres in this same district where the German Infantry averaged 30 miles a day during the whole five days of actual operations. In the same manoeuvres, 1892, the Cavalry actually marched from 60 to 70 miles on one day and about 50 on the others, whilst patrols covered as much as 120 in the twenty-four hours. The following year the Corps Artillery on one occasion marched 62 miles on end. There was no excitement of war to keep the men up, and anyhow this does not help the horses.

Compare also Lord Lake's marches against the Mahrattas in 1803-4.

Chapter 5

The Battles of Jena & Auerstadt

Whilst the Prussians lay shivering through the cold night of the 13th, without great-coats, and not daring to touch the fuel and food[1] the villages in the vicinity most amply afforded them, the French, under Napoleon's personal direction, were busily engaged in improving the track to the Landgrafenberg from the town of Jena below, and dragging up the guns of the V Corps and the Guards by main force. In the early hours of the morning a dense fog settled down over the plateau, effectually screening the two adversaries from one another. Fortunate, indeed, for the French that it was so, for otherwise the extraordinary target they presented could not conceivably have escaped the observation of the Prussian outposts, for close behind the line of the French pickets, were massed some 25,000 men, with many horses and guns, the bulk of Lannes' Corps and the Imperial Guards, not at regulation distances, but crowded breast against knapsack, as close as men could stand.

From the Prussian position to the centre of this mass was barely 1,200 yards, and what its fate must have been had the Prussian Artillery opened upon it, it is difficult to conceive.

Not even Napoleon's strategy, which had so far worked without apparent hindrance, could well have averted disas-

---

1. This is the received tradition and applies to the bulk of the Prussian troops, as we have seen above some of them did break out and plunder.

ter, for had Napoleon been swept away in the debacle which must have ensued, his Marshals were in no position to carry out his design, the essence of which they were so far from apprehending.

But the fog (which under somewhat similar conditions at Spion Kop proved our undoing), in Napoleon's case became the means of his salvation. As soon as there was light enough to see, not a moment was lost in pushing on the outpost line of Lannes' Corps (backed up by the nearest guns) to engage the enemy; and soon a brisk roll of musketry, interspersed with the detonations of artillery, gave warning to the Prussian Headquarters that the attack had begun.

Prince Hohenlohe, however, was in no frame of mind to heed the warning. As a consequence of the unfortunate interruption of his projected offensive on the previous afternoon, he had settled down into that most dangerous frame of mind, in which a man refuses to accept anything beyond the responsibility for the execution of direct orders.

Throughout the night Tauenzien had been reporting the sound of road-making operations, of firing at the outposts, and all the noises indicating the movement of large bodies of the enemy; it was never the custom of the French to work silently. Equally disquieting reports from the Saxons in the Isserstedter Forest to the south, and from Holtzendorf's patrols towards Camburg and Dornburg on the north, also came in, but he paid no attention to them. Headquarters had told him there was to be no battle next day, and as far as he was concerned, he meant to avoid provoking one. If the enemy chose to do so, at least he would not go half-way to meet him. At length, however, about 7 a.m. the firing became too general for the Prince to disregard it any longer, so he mounted and rode towards the camp of Grawert's Division. Here he found the men already fallen in, but the tents still standing. He rode through the lines telling every one there was to be no serious fighting that day, and when at length he found that in response to Tauenzien's urgent orders for reinforcements a portion of the troops were already marching out, he lost his temper completely, and sent his Staff galloping after them to bring them back. Fortunately, Grawert himself arrived and succeeded in convincing his Chief of the necessity of sending help to his hard-pressed comrade in front. It was well that he did so, for in the meantime the fighting on the outpost line had been growing in severity. The supports of the pickets had been brought up, and were firing volleys into the fog in the direction disclosed by the flashes of the guns, and though neither side could really see each other, case on the one hand and volleys on the other were doing heavy damage. The Saxons, considerably outnumbered, and everywhere locally overlapped, were falling back towards the Dornburg. Before 8.30 a.m. Lutzeroda and Closewitz were already in French hands, and shortly afterwards the crest running south from the Dornburg towards the Isserstedter Forest *(the key of the whole position)* was also occupied by them. *Thus by resolutely turning to account the temporary advantage which the fog had afforded him, Napoleon had already won the cardinal point of the whole battle.* Not only had he gained space for deployment, but the advantage of concealment for the massing of his reserves had also become his, and no one knew better how to profit by it.

Meanwhile, Holtzendorf's detachment isolated in wide cantonments around Rödigen and without orders, hearing the heavy firing, had fallen in, and though much delayed by the fog, was marching to the sound of the guns, his Light Troops well in advance as a protection. In the fog these ran full against the skirmishers of St. Hilaire's Division of Soult's Corps, also pressing on to the plateau to gain ground for deployment.

In the first encounter, Holtzendorf's men proved fully equal in individual fighting force to the French, and without much difficulty drove the latter out of the Heiligenholtz. Covered by their skirmishers and guided only by the bullets and the sounds of the firing, Holtzendorf deployed his command into line and moved to the attack in echelon, right in front with the regularity of the parade ground. So far, indeed, the Prussian drill-ground training had not failed them, but now began a succession of disasters. The Cavalry Brigade of Soult's Corps (8th Hussars, 11th and 16th Chasseurs) emerging suddenly upon the Saxon Light Horse, covering the left of the Prussian line, and catching them in the fog at a disadvantage, fairly rode over them.

Pursuers and pursued then dashed down upon the following Infantry, who did not see them until too late to avoid the encounter, with the result that a couple of battalions were completely demoralized. Almost at the same moment the French Infantry, heavily reinforced, pressed forward to the attack, and the Saxons, overwhelmingly outnumbered were compelled to fall back. Two battalions only (separated earlier by the fog, which now, however, about 10 a.m., was beginning to lift) pursued their way unmolested towards Vierzehn-heiligen where their subsequent appearance at an opportune moment caused some disturbance to the Emperor's main attack, but only enough to show what Holtzendorf's men might have done had they but started half an hour earlier.

Meanwhile, Tauenzien in obedience to orders received, was withdrawing his shattered battalions towards Klein Röm-stedt and rallying other detachments, which in the shrouding mist had been unable to find him. Two battalions, however, had been separated from him in the French attack, and had retreated into the Isserstedter Forest, where they rallied on General Niesemeuschel's brigade (Saxons). In the confusion of this retreat, no one thought of leaving garrisons in the villages of Krippendorf and Vierzehnheiligen, a most unfortunate oversight, as the sequel will show.

The French were pressing in pursuit, though not too closely, for Tauenzien still showed a bold front in retreat, and the Gettkandt Hussars delivered a bold and well-timed charge upon the French right, the leading regiments of which had already suffered severely, and, as a consequence, one of them, the 17th Light, had to be relieved, and was not brought into action again that day. Behind the advancing screen of skirmishers Lannes' Corps was executing a change of position, half-left, which brought its right wing on to the village of Krippendorf, but left Vierzehnheiligen for the moment unoccupied, and behind Lannes' again the Guards were moving down the slopes of the Dornburg to a slight hollow which sheltered them from observation. The Emperor himself was busily engaged in getting together a big battery of heavy guns, but only succeeded in collecting 18, *viz.*, 4 eight-pounders from the V Corps, and 14 from the Imperial Guard.[1] The exact number is worth noting, to compare with the big batteries he subsequently took to forming, 100 guns and upwards, at Wagram, Leipzig, etc.

The fog was now lifting in earnest (about 10 a.m.), and the firing on this part of the field had ceased for the moment, when suddenly from the east a heavy outburst of musketry and artillery was heard. This proceeded from the engagement between Holtzendorf and St. Hilaire, already alluded to. On hearing it, Napoleon stopped the attack which Lannes was preparing upon Vierzehnheiligen and detached a Brigade (Vedel) in the direction of Lehesten to cover his right flank.

This would have been the moment for Hohenlohe to seize, had he been in his proper place, well up to the front. But he had contented himself with remaining with Grawert's Division, to the deployment of which he had given a tardy consent. But, as the roar of the firing drew nearer, his fighting instinct reasserted itself, and about 8 a.m. he decided to take his share in the coming fight. He therefore dispatched a note to Rüchel at Weimar, begging him to spare what troops he could to act as a support.

After some groping (for the fog had locally and momentarily thickened), the tracks of the. Cavalry, which had al-

---

1. Foucart, p. 665.

ready formed line facing in the direction of Vierzehnheiligen, were discovered and followed up. As soon as the whole command was united, the Prince dispatched his squadrons towards Vierzehnheiligen as an advance guard, and then addressed himself to the more congenial task of superintending the deployment of the Infantry and correcting its intervals and dressing.

The Cavalry force consisted of 19 Squadrons and a battery and a half of Horse Artillery, and were joined in their advance on their left, by the 10 Squadrons of Gettkandt Hussars, who had just rallied after their first brilliant charge, on their right by 10 Squadrons of Prussian Dragoons and Cuirassiers and 6 Squadrons of Saxons with one Horse Artillery battery, making 45 Squadrons in all, or twelve more than Seydlitz commanded at Rossbach; but there was, unfortunately, no worthy successor of that immortal leader at hand to guide them.

Arrived at the village of Vierzehnheiligen, this imposing array split into two almost equal wings and was preparing to charge the few Light guns and the swarms of skirmishers (all for the moment that they could see before them), when a sudden interruption on their right brought the whole to a more or less disorderly halt. It must be remembered that their front was over a mile long, and was, moreover, broken by the village. The fog still lay in patches in the low ground, which was marshy in many places. But all Seydlitz's precautions in these cases had now been omitted.[1]

The interruption arose from the following circumstances: Ney, if he had ever received his orders, had certainly never studied them, but hearing the firing on the Landgrafenberg he had immediately called his advance guard under arms, and choosing the western exit from the town, in order, as he said in his subsequent report to the Emperor,

---

1. See *Cavalry, Past and Future,* by the Author.

"to have at least a chance of participating in the glorious events which were preparing," was now moving upon the extreme left of Lannes in the hollows south of Vierzehnheiligen.[1] His two Cavalry Regiments (3rd Hussars, 10th Chasseurs) were leading. Seeing a Prussian battery on a slight knoll in front of them, his men dashed straight at it, and surging far beyond it, found themselves on the flank of the Prussian Cavalry line. Without a moment's hesitation they wheeled in upon them, and there ensued a confused succession of squadron charges, as a net result of which the Prussian right gave way. This movement transplanted itself from squadron to squadron and by degrees the whole line withdrew, thus uncovering the advance of Grawert's deployed Division. This, however, not until their ranks had been considerably thinned and their horses unsteadied by the heavy fire of the big French battery, and the swarms of skirmishers, now streaming into and occupying the village with its adjacent gardens and orchards.

Whilst the Cavalry was clearing the front, Grawert's Division remained halted to correct their dressing, and to allow the last of the fog to disperse, and Hohenlohe occupied the time in haranguing the men, who were in excellent spirits at the prospect of at length getting a chance to show their mettle. The previous checks at Saalfeld and Schleiz, though the troops therein concerned had been almost destroyed as units, had only served to raise the fighting temper of the remainder of the Army to that point at which troops become most dangerous. So for the moment fortune seemed to smile upon the Prussian Arms, and when the well-known drill-ground command, "Advance in echelon from the left" rang out, the troops moved off, bands playing and colours flying, with a precision and swing "not often attained even on the parade ground," as all eye-witnesses testify.

---

1. Foucart, p. 646.

Fortunately for them, the Emperor's big battery could not be brought to bear upon them, as a roll in the ground intervened, but the Light Divisional Batteries of Lannes' Corps had galloped out well to the front, and now sent a tempest of case in their teeth. His Infantry also had just succeeded in settling itself for defence in the houses and gardens of the village, and from every window and hedgerow, a sharp skirmishing fire rattled against them. Had the village remained unoccupied all might yet have been well, for the Prussian troops were quite sufficiently drilled for the passage of such obstacles, and it was doubtless under the impression that it was still empty that the advance had been ordered. But when it became clear to the Staff that the reverse was the case, they hesitated as to what course to pursue, for the attack of villages formed no part of the duties of the Line troops. This had always been reserved in Frederick's day for the "Freisehaaren," which now no longer existed, and the Fusiliers intended to take their place were already employed elsewhere.

At short musket range of the village, therefore, the leading echelon was halted, and line formed upon it with the utmost accuracy. Each battalion opened fire by company volleys as its dressing was completed, whilst a howitzer battery was brought up to set the houses on fire; which it did within a very few minutes.

So far so good. The French Light troops outside the garden walls had everywhere fallen back, and his Staff now pressed upon Hohenlohe to order the advance to continue. But, unfortunately, in vain, although even Massenbach is reported to have said to him, that to stand fast meant certain destruction. Apparently he still felt himself too weak for a further attack, and believing Rüchel to be nearer at hand than he actually was, he decided to await his arrival.

Now followed one of the most extraordinary and pitiful incidents in military history. This line of magnificent Infantry, some 20,000 strong, stood out in the open for two whole hours whilst exposed to the merciless case and skirmishing fire of the French, who behind the garden walls offered no mark at all for their return fire. In places the fronts of the companies were only marked by individual files still loading and firing, whilst all their comrades lay dead and dying around them.

Thus the time drew on: unfortunately, as credible testimony records, Grawert had formed no second line at all, and even before his advance began, Ney's Infantry had already penetrated into the Isserstedter Forest and destroyed the connection between the Saxon and Prussian commands. To close this gap Dykerren's Brigade, made up of the troops so heavily shaken at Saalfeld and Schleitz, had been ordered up, as well as what reserves the Saxons could muster. Hence about 1 p.m. every available soldier of Hohenlohe's command, except Tauenzien's shattered contingent, stood in a single line, no fresh troops in reserve within sight or call. Owing to causes impossible now to unravel (certainly, however, Rüchel's unwillingness formed no part of them), the latter's nearest troops were still only half-way on their road from Weimar.

Meanwhile Napoleon sat waiting *"till the battle was ripe"* and from every quarter fresh regiments were streaming in to his assistance.

Augereau had long since tackled and was holding the Saxons about *"die Schnecke"*.[1] Vedel's Brigade having learnt of the dispersal of Holtzendorf's detachment had countermarched and was now in its place with Lannes' Corps. St. Hilaire, having left a few patrols to follow up Holtzendorf, had wheeled his Division to its left, and was marching down upon the extreme Prussian left, while Murat with all his squadrons was formed up in rear of the Guard, and the main bodies of Ney's and Soult's Corps were rapidly massing on Murat's flanks.

---

1. *Die Schnecke* was the name locally given to the zigzags of the Weimar road leading up to the plateau.

Exclusive of the troops already engaged, the Emperor had, therefore, not less than 75,000 men immediately ready to his hand, and might safely await the inevitable debacle of the enemy in his front. It came at last, about 1 p.m., beginning with the extreme left. The Prussian Cavalry in support threw themselves gallantly but disconnectedly against the enemy to cover the withdrawal, but met by fresh French troops, both horse and foot, could effect but little beyond a gain of invaluable minutes. At last Prince Hohenlohe yielded to the Inevitable, and commenced an orderly retreat. The men, however, were too utterly spent to respond, and under the pursuit of the French skirmishers, and the charges of the Divisional Cavalry, practically every formation was broken, except the square of the Saxon battalion, "von Winkel," in which Hohenlohe himself had taken shelter. This square beat off by its steady bearing and fire every Cavalry charge directed against it.

To complete the catastrophe, only one further misfortune was needed, and at this moment Massenbach, that evil genius of the Prussian Army, was on his way to ensure its happening. He had remained with Prince Hohenlohe almost to the last minute (for whatever his faults, physical cowardice at any rate was not one of them), and had then been despatched to hasten Rüchel's arrival. He met the latter somewhere in the vicinity of Frankendorf, and in reply to the query in what direction help could best be rendered, he replied, "now only through Capellendorf"; whereas, in the state of affairs actually existing, all further offensive was foredoomed to failure, and only the occupation of the strong defensive section afforded by the Sulzbach between Capellendorf and Hammerstedt, behind which the scattered troops might reunite, could be of any avail. It was not a question of holding it indefinitely—that, of course, was out of the question. But the sun sets on October 14 about 5.30, and till then the 12,000 bayonets with their battalion guns might well have held their own, with consequence of far-reaching benefit to the whole Prussian cause.

Rüchel had been left at Weimar to rally the Duke of Weimar's command dispatched into the Thuringian Forest. He had received Hohenlohe's request for such troops as he could spare about 9 a.m., to which, like Blücher on a later occasion, he had replied that he would come with his whole command.

This command was considerably scattered, but a little after 10 a.m. the head of his column was on the march. Near Umpferstedt he received a second note from the Prince, to whom again he notified the approach of his whole little Army, and in answer he immediately gave orders to hasten the march. It was probably the arrival of this note (it has never to my knowledge been traced) which led Hohenlohe to the unfortunate decision to postpone the attack on Vierzehnheiligen. It being only six miles from Weimar to the village in question, the column might well have reached the ground and deployed by 12 noon. A modern Prussian Division would have easily effected this over this country in ninety minutes, but in fact, at 2 p.m., i.e., after four hours, the head of the column was only just reaching Capellendorf, and to this day no one has been able to suggest any explanation of this extraordinary dilatoriness. The command included some celebrated old Prussian regiments, "Alt Larisch," "Winning," "Wedel" but Rüchel had unfortunately disorganized them all by ordering them to form only two deep during the coming campaign, and to group all the superfluous third ranks into special battalions. But this, though always given as one of the causes of their ultimate failure, need hardly be quoted seriously as an excuse, if, indeed, any excuse for failing to achieve the impossible is needed. In compliance with Massenbach's suggestion, the head of the column bent off towards Capellendorf. Leaving three battalions behind as a reserve, together with the battalion guns, for which the ground beyond the Sulzbach was obviously unfavourable, the remainder filed through the village and deployed in the meadows beyond at the foot of the Sperlingberg, which rises some 150 feet above the stream at a moderate slope. Some French skirmishers are said to have already crowned its summit.

This deployment completed, the advance began in echelons of three battalions each, from the centre. A Horse Artillery battery accompanied the right flank, and over and above Rüchel's own squadrons a considerable number of units escaped from the battlefield rallied further on his right.

Hardly had the line stepped off when a number of French Light batteries unlimbered on the hill and opened fire on the advancing ranks with case. But the men pressed forward in perfect order, and the enemy's guns limbered up and retired at the gallop. The Prussians followed, still preserving their admirable bearing, and for the moment with no enemy in sight, when suddenly a whole dense swarm of Infantry, extending as far as the eye could reach, and interspersed with batteries, arose above the edge of the plateau. Then a terrific fire-fight ensued. It lasted about fifteen minutes. At last the Prussians, unable single-handed to cope with both Infantry and Artillery, began to break backwards. Many battalions lost at least half their men, and the Cavalry dashed forward most gallantly to relieve them. But they were met by fresh French squadrons chiefly of Lannes' Corps, and the whole mass drifted down upon the Infantry, who were swept away by the combined weight of both friend and foe. In about half an hour the whole affair was over, and the last closed battalion had practically ceased to exist. Then Murat at the head of his almost intact command took up the pursuit and continued it practically up to the Gates of Erfurt.

Hohenlohe, having renounced in obedience to what he believed to be the intentions of Headquarters, the opportunity of inflicting a smart repulse on the advance guard of Lannes' Corps, a stroke well within the limits of initiative belonging to a rear guard commander, had only one possible course open to him on the morning of October 14, and this he omitted to take.

The reports he received from his outposts were ample enough to warn him of the danger his force was bound to incur by delay, and he had it well within his power to call on all his troops, including Rüchel at Weimar, to be ready to move off at daybreak and concentrate between Vierzehnheiligen and Alt Gönna, for the fog did not begin to settle down till just before dawn, and if the French could find energy enough to march all night and reconnoitre and improve the paths leading up out of the river gorge to the plateau, his Staff might at least have done the same.

The fog then would have helped him as much as in fact it hampered his actual movements, for in view of the gap in his line of outposts about Camburg and Dornburg, his position was untenable the moment daylight sufficed to reveal his intentions; as matters actually stood it would have given him just the concealment he required, and leaving the rendezvous say at 6, half an hour before the Emperor gave the signal of attack, his main body would have been well clear of the dangerous point about Alt Gönna and Lehesten before St. Hilaire's Division arrived on the scene. Napoleon's concentration on the plateau would then have been a blow in the air, and much time would have been lost in reconnoitring the true state of affairs, for the Emperor was still dominated by the idea that the decision really lay at Weimar. Had the King of Prussia received the intelligence of Hohenlohe's approach, the whole face of the battle of Auerstädt would have been changed, as we shall presently see, and there can be little doubt that the Prussian Army, still as a fighting whole, would have crushed Davout and marched over him to the passages of the Unstrutt at Freiburg and Taucha as originally intended.

But having made this initial error, which nothing could redeem, he then continued to make in succession every error which the fortune of the day threw open to him.

It was irrational with only 42,000 men within call to risk a decision at all, more particularly when 8,000 of his

153

men had already been uselessly expended, at Lutzeroda, and Closewitz, and another 5,000 dispersed about Alt Gönna; but having decided to fight, the least he could have done would have been to have waited for Rüchel to join him before advancing, not after the fight had already commenced. Where he stood to fight on this open and rolling plateau was almost unimportant, any one ridge was as good as another; but the essence of good tactics on such a plain would have been to have made the most of the concealment for masses which the ground afforded, and to have met the French attacks with volleys and cold steel in the Peninsula manner, on the crest of the ridges. But to attack downhill in the full sweep of his enemy's artillery fire was courting destruction then, just as it would be now.

It is interesting to follow out what might have happened, when the fog lifted sufficiently to disclose the whole situation, had it only occurred to someone to leave garrisons in Vierzehnheiligen and Krippendorf as Tauenzien's troops withdrew beyond them, for a more promising opportunity for a Cavalry charge has seldom offered itself than at this moment. There on the Prussian left stood a mass of squadrons which might have been launched down upon the French skirmishers and Light Artillery and ridden them down from flank to flank, returning afterwards round the right, thus taking those battalions and squadrons of Ney's advance guard still outside of the Isserstedter Forest in reverse, and effectually clearing the way for the further advance of the line. No doubt the Imperial Guard would have sufficed ultimately to bring this advance to a standstill, but a good hour had still to elapse before the arrival of French reinforcements once again gave the numerical preponderance into Napoleon's hands, and even then a retreat might have been initiated under very different conditions to those under which it actually took place. But what a difference defeat after such a temporary advantage would have made on the *moral* of the whole Army and even of the Nation during the ensuing years! No one then could have laid the blame for defeat on the tactical method adopted, but the investigation with its causes would have had to be pressed home deeper and carried out to where it actually lay.

This will become clearer when we have followed the course of the battle which was simultaneously raging only twelve miles away, till when it will be better to postpone the fuller consideration of the tactical problems the incidents of this fateful day suggest.

THE BATTLE OF AUERSTADT

About 6 a.m. the principal Army recommenced its march along the Kösen road, Schmettau's Division leading, preceded by a squadron of cavalry as scouts. The fog lay thick over the country, and occasioned confusion in the columns from the very start.

The Light Division under Blücher, with 28 squadrons of Hussars and Dragoons, should have formed the advance guard, but they had only reached their bivouacs, south of Auerstadt, after a long day's work as flankers to the main body, about 2 a.m., and though Blücher himself had urged all haste, they found themselves cut off by the confusion reigning in the streets of Auerstadt, into which other troops were already pouring, and apparently, having reached their ground during the night, they did not know that the stream over the bridge immediately beyond the village, where the block began, was easily fordable both above and below. Actually, the command was split in half, and only two Cavalry Regiments, the "Irwing" Dragoons and a battalion of Blücher Hussars, succeeded in forcing their way through the press, the remainder, under General von Oswald, never regained touch with their commander during the day.

155

Meanwhile, the Dragoons forming the point of Schmettau's Division had come into collision with some hostile scouts near Poppel and driven them back on Taugwitz, but the fog still hid the enemy's movements, and to clear up the situation the Duke of Brunswick who, in face of the enemy, had once more recovered his energy and determination, had detached the bulk of the squadrons under Schmettau's command for reconnoitring purposes. At this moment Blücher rode up. Seeing the latter, the Duke handed over to him the remainder of Schmettau's Cavalry, not without remonstrance on the latter's part, and sent him forward towards the Ranzen Hills on the north of the main road, ordering Schmettau to halt until further information could be secured. In the fog, Blücher only found seven squadrons altogether and was moving off, when heavy firing broke out from the direction of Hassenhausen, where the point of the advance guard had unexpectedly come upon a French battery with Infantry escort, and had been received with case shot. This was the advance guard of Davout's Corps, 2 battalions, 1 squadron and 1 battery, which in obedience of Napoleon's orders, received about 3 a.m., was moving forward on Apolda. But the fog concealed their weakness, and Blücher, who about this time had reached the summit of the Ranzen Hill, heard only the discharge of the guns, and nearly rode into a deployed French line, which through the mist he had mistaken for a hedgerow. Rightly abstaining from engaging himself with unbroken Infantry in unknown strength, he sent back for more troops, both Infantry and Cavalry, and for a moment the engagement came to a standstill.

Davout had received his orders from Berthier at 3 a.m.— they were dated 10 p.m., Jena—and having in obedience to the instructions sent to him by the Emperor, at 3 p.m. the previous afternoon, made every preparation for an immediate advance, his troops were under arms about 6 a.m., and at once commenced their march on Apolda, the destination assigned to them in the aforesaid order.

Thanks, however, to the fog, confusion arose in arranging the departure of the several Divisions, and as a consequence his leading Division, Gudin, was now about to find itself in a position of such imminent peril that but for the fog it must have been annihilated, for Blücher, whilst waiting for reinforcements, had worked round the French right flank, and when these arrived, though with only three squadrons where he had expected ten, he immediately charged, and with such effect that Davout had to take shelter in the squares which were rapidly formed, and the French squadrons, only three in number, were driven from the field. Against perfectly unshaken Infantry, however, the Cavalry could accomplish nothing, and after renewing the charge a second time—in which Blücher had his horse shot under him, they fell back in considerable disorder, having, however, delayed the French deployment and given time for Schmettau's Division to clear the village of Auerstadt and commence its formation for attack. This, however, was interfered with by a somewhat unusual incident. As Blücher's squadrons fell back, a horse-artillery battery (Merkatz) remained in its position covering the retreat, and its fire inflicted considerable punishment on the leading battalions of Friant's Division, which now (9.30 a.m.) was rapidly approaching. Some French Chasseur squadrons were sent against this battery which they rode into for the moment, but then in the fog they blundered right in between the two lines of Schmettau's Division engaged in deploying, with the result that in the confusion the second line of Infantry fired into the backs of the first line in front of them. The French Cavalry were ultimately driven off by a charge of Schmettau's Divisional Cavalry, and pursued in the direction of the Spielberg, where Blücher's squadrons were then rallying, but unfortunately for Schmettau, they elected to remain with their own arm for the rest of the day, so that when at length Schmettau's Division commenced its advance, it was without any accompanying squadrons.

This, however, was not the only unfortunate consequence which arose out of this accidental intrusion of the French Chasseurs between the Prussian lines.

The Duke of Brunswick, who had been watching the deployment of the Division, and had already sent off most of his Staff to call up reinforcements, pointing out the heights south of Hassenhausen as the direction the fresh troops on arrival were to take, was with his Quarter-Master-General Scharnhorst, just south of the trees along the high road, when he heard the firing of Schmettau's second line, referred to above, and struck by the direction from which the sound came over, he ordered Scharnhorst to ride over and find out the cause, adding, "I make you personally responsible for all which happens over there." Owing to the relations between the two being somewhat strained, the consequence of the events which had occurred during the previous days, Scharnhorst took this order as a hint to keep out of the Duke's way with results absolutely fatal to the Prussian cause, when shortly afterwards the Duke was mortally wounded.

At length, Schmettau's Division moved forward, sweeping the French skirmishers before it, but the latter had had time to occupy Hassenhausen strongly, and that village now played the same part in the battle as Vierzehnheiligen at Jena.

Against it the Prussian Infantry could do nothing, and whilst the centre was held fast in front of it, the wings swung inwards, thus exposing their outer flanks to French counter-attacks. As at Vierzehnheiligen, no one could summon up resolution enough to order a bayonet charge, and under a devastating fire the long line held on for fresh reinforcements to arrive. They came at length in the form of Wartensleben's Division, which after endless delays in the streets of Auerstadt had at length completed its deployment, and was being led forward to the heights south of the village by the Duke in person. Whilst thus engaged he received a bullet through both eyes, which of course incapacitated him from further service.

To add to the misfortune, his Staff being dispersed, there was no one to carry the news to the King, who alone could make arrangements for the exercise of the Duke's functions, for it appears that no Second in Command had been nominated.

Even when at length the news reached the King, the latter neither named a successor, nor himself took over the command. Thus at the critical moment, when victory seemed in the grasp of the Prussian Arms, fortune deserted them, and for a time the battle was allowed to work itself.

To this, however, the old line tactics did not readily adapt themselves, and the war-seasoned French troops, with Davout, Gudin, Friant and Morand at their head, were not the men to let tactical opportunities slip for want of initiative. Each fresh battalion as it arrived was thrown into the fight, with the result that presently the Prussian line began to give way, and each fraction, of the whole, locally outflanked, preserved its cohesion only at the price of tremendous sacrifices.

On the Prussian side the last closed Infantry body to be thrown into the fight was the Prince of Orange's Division. Like the others its deployment had been delayed in the passage of the village of Auerstadt; and now on its way to the front it was assailed by so many pressing appeals for help, that it broke into two halves, one half going to the left, the other to the right. Had the whole moved to the right, the result might have been different, for Blücher had again assembled a considerable number of squadrons, most of them much shaken, and by a succession of charges— made, however, without unity of command—had completely absorbed the attention of Morand's Division, now, about noon, arriving on the ground. But the raw Prussian Cavalry, of whom more than half had but little more training than our yeomanry, discouraged on finding out that charging unshaken squares was a very different matter to what they had been led to anticipate, drifted away from the action a little too soon, and the four battalions of the Prince's Division found themselves outnumbered when at length they reached the front.

The French now assumed the offensive and slowly pressed the Prussians back upon their still intact reserves under Kalckreuth, whose conduct on this occasion has ever since been held up as an example of how reserves ought not to be employed. Actually, however, as so often happens, the blame, at least in part, should be laid on other shoulders.

The total amount of reserves still in hand at this period of the battle, about 1 p.m., consisted of the Divisions of von Arnim and von Künheim, together with a brigade of Light Infantry under von Oswald.

But these were not all united under one command, for in the early hours of the fog Oswald had been sent to occupy the village of Sulza and block the passage over the Ilm at this point. Through some misunderstanding von Künheim had followed him with Hirschfeld's brigade of the line Division, and here they remained for the rest of the day, apparently forgotten or unnoticed. There remained only three brigades of Infantry, one Cavalry brigade of 15 squadrons and one horse battery (though, of course, the line battalions had their own guns) and those had been deployed by Kalckreuth along the spur of the Eckardsberg, which runs nearly due east and west across the plain towards Gernstedt—in charity one can only suppose that this took place before the fog had lifted, and it seems probable that this was actually the case. But once there, Kalckreuth felt himself compelled to remain there, "so as to be near his Majesty, and ready to execute any orders he might be pleased to convey to me." It would seem, therefore, that this immobility of the reserve was due to a misapprehension as to who was actually commanding in the battle, for whilst His Majesty was riding down the front of his battalions, Kalckreuth could hardly move off his command without the Monarch's permission. It would seem, further, that in so doing Kalckreuth was, in fact, acting in accordance with the King's wishes, for having finished his inspection, he now personally ordered some of the battalions into the fight to cover the retreat of the stragglers from Hassenhausen, issuing these orders to each battalion individually without reference to the Divisional Commander.

As these reinforcements, led up in dribblets, proved quite inadequate to arrest or rally the wreck of the first attacks now drifting back from Hassenhausen, and as the King had no idea of the strength of the enemy with whom he was engaged, and of course had not the remotest conception that only twelve miles away, Napoleon was annihilating Hohenlohe and his 42,000 men—the idea of keeping a reserve intact and withdrawing westward to rally his whole Army was by no means so blameworthy as it has generally been held to be. If Napoleon himself was coming up from Kösen and the troops in sight were only his leading corps, it was clear that the Prussians could not hope to break through at Freiburg and Laucha, but they might, reinforced by Hohenlohe make good their retreat across the Harz on Magdeburg from Buttstedt and Weimar, as ultimately a large fraction of them actually did; but, as misfortune would have it, Prince Hohenlohe's defeat had already practically closed that issue, and under the circumstances the King's order had very little result one way or the other, for long before Weimar was reached the presence of the French in Apolda was discovered, and the troops made their escape as best they could from the field, most of them going by Buttstedt.

Their resistance, however, had been so obstinate that Davout was quite unable to pursue them. Of the 26,000 men he had succeeded in bringing on the field no less than 258 officers and 6,794 men, viz., 25½ per cent., had fallen,[1] and the

1.			
1st Division	98 officers	2,181 men	=25 per cent
2nd Division	30 officers	900 men	=12 per cent
3rd Division	134 officers	3,500 men	=41 per cent
Cavalry Brigade	6 officers	213 men	=17 per cent
Totals	**258 officers**	**6,794 men**	**=25½ per cent**

3rd Division, Gudin, with 41 per cent., is perhaps the heaviest loss recorded as borne by victorious troops in so large a unit as a Division.[1] during the whole Napoleonic period. Davout estimated the Prussian loss in killed and wounded at 15,000, but though it is impossible to check these figures, owing to the loss of so many regimental records and the general confusion of the retreat, this is obviously far too high, for as Lettow Vorbeck points out (p. 408, Vol. I.) that would make 40 per cent, of the troops actually seriously engaged, and the accounts of eye-witnesses recently published in the *Urkundliche Forschungen,* though they show the punishment to have been severe, indicate nothing to justify such a heavy gross percentage.

The actual sequence of events was briefly this: Gudin brought 8,000 men onto the field, of which 6,400 were presently engaged against 7,700 men of Schmettau's Division. Then Friant arrived with 9,400, against which Wartensleben was opposed with 7,800. Lastly, Morand arrived, in the nick of time to meet the Cavalry charges and the advance of the Prince of Orange's Division, bringing about 3,100 men to either flank. The numbers of muskets engaged were, therefore, at each stage of the action approximately equal; and though the French troops in Hassenhausen must have suffered considerably less than their comrades in the open, the Prussian loss must have been fairly uniform along the whole front, and would vary in the Divisions with the duration of exposure to fire.

Eight thousand, therefore, would be a fair computation for the losses which determined the issue of the fight, and 2,000 for those who fell in the retreat, and if this estimate is allowed, the shooting of the Prussians appears to have been well up to the average, for since no fresh ammunition reached the front, the average expenditure cannot have exceeded the amount of ammunition actually carried, or 60 rounds a man, which would give in round numbers 1,200,000 bullets for 7,000 hits,

1. Augereau's Corps at Eylau lost 57 per cent., but it can hardly be said to have been borne by victorious troops.

say 170 per French casualty. A certain proportion, too, must be assigned to the fire of the battalion guns and the Cavalry, and this would bring the figure down to 1 hit for 200 rounds, the accepted average throughout the Napoleonic period.

The point is well worth making, for as usual in a beaten army, the want of musketry training of the troops, and the indifferent quality of the weapons supplied to them, was freely brought forward to account for the Prussian defeat.[1]

It is curious to notice how history thus repeats itself The outcry always arises, yet history when closely examined shows that the quality of the arms and the musketry training of the men has very little to do with the final results, and very generally victory falls to the Army with the worst Infantry weapon. Thus the Americans during the Rebellion though armed often with only old shotguns, and practically no artillery, more than held their own against the well-armed British. The Southerners in the American Civil War were generally far worse armed than the Northerners, and the musketry training much the same; the French incomparably better armed in 1870 than the Germans; the Turks better than the Russians in 1877; the British than the Boers in 1881, and possibly in 1899; and, finally, the Russian, European Army than the Japanese in 1904. The real truth of the matter is that victory is the product of the efficiency of the three Arms, of the skill of the leader, and of the discipline of the men. If the discipline of the men suffices for the execution of the leader's design, and he knows how to combine the action of the three Arms to the

---

1. Even Clausewitz, in his *Nachrichten-über Preussen* did not hesitate to assert twenty years after the War, that "the Prussian muskets were the worst in Europe," an assertion that Jany, in the *Urkundliche Forschungen* has since entirely refuted. *See* part 5, p. 33, *et seq.* The old Prussian musket had been spoiled by the substitution of a very straight stock designed to make it easier to carry at the old "shoulder arms," and was about 30 per cent, behind the French musket in accuracy at 100 and 200 paces. On the other hand, it was 10 per cent, better at 300 and 400, and thanks to the conical touch-hole, introduced about 1780, and the cylindrical iron ramrod, it could be loaded and fired about twice to the French once.

best advantage, then his Army will always find targets which they cannot miss, and tasks which they can easily accomplish. But the Art of the Leader consists in so judging his men that he does not call upon them for tasks above their strength, in other words, "in adapting the means at hand to the attainment of the object in view, "and thus we arrive by another method at Moltke's original definition of the "Art of War."

BERNADOTTE'S CONDUCT

No account of these two battles can be complete without an allusion to the extraordinary failure of the I Corps to participate in either.

Bernadotte was with Murat and Davout at Naumburg when the orders of Berthier, dated 3 p.m., 13th, were received, by which the former was ordered to Dornburg, and the latter told to stand fast unless heavy firing was heard from Jena until later instructions should reach him. As his Corps had been marching all day, he took shelter behind the promise of later orders and halted his men, along the road to Dornburg, on the right bank of the Saale with the tail of the column in Naumburg, where he himself passed the night with Davout. There seems no doubt that in the general disposition he had been overlooked, for when the orders dated 10 p.m., Jena, were despatched to Davout (received at 3 a.m.), directing him to march on Apolda, the Major-General added: "If Marshal Bernadotte is still with you, you can march together, but the Emperor hopes he will be in the position indicated to him at Dornburg." Now no position had been indicated to Bernadotte, hence he concluded that some order had missed him, and though this note to Davout must have effectively covered his responsibility had he acted on it, he decided to march to Dornburg. Had he acted with energy on his arrival at Dornburg his presence there would have been more effective than his presence at Auerstadt, hence he does not seem to be seriously to blame. Unfortunately for his reputation, however, he did not act with anything approaching energy, but carried out his march so tardily that he failed to reach either field in time to render assistance.

By the time he had reached his assigned station, the fog had cleared, and it appears that he was fully informed as to the progress of the fight at Auerstadt, but no specific order from the Emperor reached him, and he determined to march on Apolda, again as good a direction as he could have chosen, but his march was conducted with such slowness that he only reached that spot at 4 p.m., having taken nearly six hours to cover eight miles, and nothing in the nature of the defiles to be overcome exists or existed to justify this delay. It is said that the Emperor had actually decided to court-martial him, and feeling in the Army ran so high that he would certainly have been convicted, but at the last moment, in view of his relationship by marriage to the Imperial family, the Emperor relented.

One thing is quite certain, *viz.*, that in going to Dornburg instead of staying with Davout, he showed a better grasp of the Imperial idea than his many critics. His troops being already on the Dornburg road, they could only have followed Davout into action, and must have arrived too late to prevent his defeat had the Prussians only pressed home their advantage. But as the Emperor viewed the situation, i.e., that Davout had only a rear-guard in front of him, and he himself had the bulk of the Prussian Army in his front, what happened to Davout mattered nothing at all, as long as he, the Emperor, won a decisive victory at Jena, and therefore, in accordance with his favourite axiom, "You can never be too strong at the decisive point," Bernadotte was right in marching by the shortest line to the main decision.

It cannot be insisted upon too often that Napoleon aimed only at economy of force, i.e. of human life, essentially on the whole transaction, and provided that he was successful in this, the fate of a detachment troubled him not at all.

A subordinate, therefore, was bound under all circumstances to get the last ounce of fight out of his command; and he had no right to complain whatever the odds might be that he found himself called upon to encounter.

It is a hard doctrine; and we cannot wonder if now and again the troops sacrificed felt themselves betrayed.

CHAPTER 6

Conclusion & Comments

Whilst I subscribe entirely to the importance attributed by the French General Staff to this new interpretation of the Napoleonic method, which in the above pages I have endeavoured to elucidate, I confess that it has always seemed to me unfortunate that the Jena Campaign has been so frequently chosen as the example of its highest development.

To me it has always seemed that Napoleon was still only feeling his way with his new invention, and as yet had not learnt to trust to it as implicitly as in his subsequent campaigns. He was like an inventor with a new design, the full potentiality of which he has not had time to develop. If this is not so, how are we to account for his hesitations and feverish mental activity on the night of October 11-12, when the news that the King was in Erfurt, led him to the conclusion that he meant to stay there, and as a consequence was certain to be found and defeated somewhere in the near vicinity of Weimar?

The essence of the Napoleonic doctrine as I apprehend it, is *that it is useless to manoeuvre until you have "a fixed 'point" about which to revolve.* The action of the *"Avante Garde Generale"* creates the fixed point, and only when that Advance Guard has got its teeth in, and holds the enemy in a bulldog grip, is the certainty attained that he will make no further movement, good, bad, or indifferent. The principal danger (as evidenced in the case of Moltke's several attempts to out-manoeuvre the French Army during the first days of August, 1870, lay in the possibility of the enemy making some mistake too gross ever to have entered the head of his opponent.

Now, on October 11, the French Advance Guard had not taken a firm hold of its adversary at all—only scouts and spies had observed him, and these, however much they may see, or however promptly they may report, can exercise no material holding power at all.

They could not, and they did not in this instance, prevent the Prussians moving as they pleased, and the movement they actually undertook would have taken them beyond the sweep of Napoleon's manoeuvre altogether, but for a series of blunders and delays too inconceivable to have presented themselves as possibilities to the Emperor's mind.

Now, as between two fairly-matched armies, a battle resolves itself into a struggle of endurance, physical, mental and psychic, between the two Commanders, the primary advantage of the Napoleonic method is, that it relieves the man who adopts it of all necessity for unnecessary physical or mental exertion, and thus places both his body and his mind at the disposal of his Will in their highest possible efficiency. An exhausted body and troubled mind are but poor instruments for even the most powerful Will to work with. Had Napoleon fully trusted his new creation, he would, I submit, have hesitated to set it in motion on such entirely insufficient information as lay before him on the night of October 11-12. The fact that the King was in Erfurt on the 11th proved nothing as to where he might be on the 13th and 14th; and being in the midst of his battalion square of 200,000 men, Napoleon was practically invulnerable both in flank and rear, therefore there was no need to worry about what the Prussians were doing until the continuation of his march *compelled the latter to attack him*.

The Prussians remaining, in fact, in entire ignorance of

the French movements as proved by their location of the camp about Capellendorf, i.e., facing south-west, the actual movements of Napoleon's Army cannot be said to have influenced their decisions at all. They would have moved towards the Duke of Würtemberg in any case, whatever the French might have done. Hence if on the night of the 11th the Emperor had recognized that the information at his disposal was insufficient as a foundation for a manoeuvre having a decisive battle for its object, and had continued his march along the three great roads in his normal formation, the result would have been that when the two convergent lines of march met (as they must have done near Weiszenfels), the whole Army would have been far better in hand for his ultimate manoeuvre than events actually found it, and he himself would have been fresher in mind and body for the coming decision. The phrase, *"Enfin le voile est déchiré"* betrays his mental unrest very completely.

His men, too, would have been spared much unnecessary marching, and some considerable confusion; night marches are never a good preparation for a coming battle, yet Ney, Soult and the Reserve Cavalry were on their legs almost the whole of the night of October 13-14.

By the original orders for the night of October 11-12, Lannes and Augereau would have marched on the right bank of the Saale, with the river between them and their enemy, but the amended orders threw them upon the left bank from Kahla to Jena; and it is interesting to think out what might have happened had the Prussians suddenly acted on Scharnhorst's idea, and decided to cross over the river and attack the French in flank, on this particular day.

Assume that during the afternoon of the 11th the Prussian Headquarters had ordered, say Blücher, to unite sixty out of the available eighty squadrons and cross the Saale at Camburg and Dornburg, whilst some light troops held those villages for them to fall back upon; Hohenlohe to move to Jena; Main

Army from its camps about Umpferstedt on Lobeda; and the Duke of Weimar from Ilmenau over the mountains on Rudolstadt–Kahla. Allowing for the usual delays in executing orders in the Prussian Army, it would seem that about 4 p.m., just as Augereau's leading Division was filing over the Kahla Bridge, they would have been attacked in rear by Weimar's Advance Guard of Cavalry and Light Infantry, whilst Lannes would have found himself face to face with the Duke of Brunswick and Prince Hohenlohe (say 90,000 men), with his retreat cut off by the precipitous defile formed by the river. Since, in fact, Tauenzien's and Grawert's Divisions alone more than held Lannes' Corps in check until Ney's daring disobedience of orders brought him to the latter's assistance in the battle of the 14th, what reasonable chance of success could he have had against the whole Prussian Army?

On this day, the 12th, the square formation had broken down, its constituent parts were far too scattered. Had the Prussian attack begun about noon (and thanks to their slowness it is not likely that it would have begun earlier) then Lannes' Corps must have been totally destroyed, for Augereau's leading Division only crossed the Saale at Kahla on that day after a hard and exhausting march due to counter orders received in the morning. Ney on the road from Auma to Mittel Pöllnitz, had even farther to go, and Bernadotte, Davout and Soult could not possibly have arrived before the morning of the 14th, even if Blücher and his sixty squadrons had not been able to do anything to delay their march. Probably, however, he would have ridden down Murat's squadrons of Light Cavalry and then by repeated charges and threats have compelled the two French Corps to move in mass ready to form square, precisely as, in 1813, the Allied Cavalry retarded the French march over almost the same district from the Saale to Lützen.[1]

---

1. See *The Leipsig Campaign,* by the author.

So far nothing had ever occurred in the French Army to shake its confidence in the Emperor's genius, but judging by after events, it is difficult to avoid the conclusion that the effect of the virtual destruction of a whole Corps (more particularly when commanded by Lannes) would have had a shattering effect upon the whole force, and a corresponding reaction upon the *moral* of the Prussians which might seriously have affected the issue of the whole campaign.

As we have seen during the course of the narrative, the panic in Prince Hohenlohe's command on the afternoon of the 11th effectually paralysed the energies of the Staff for the following twelve hours. But it seems equally clear, from the willingness shown by the men to be led against the enemy on the afternoon of the 13th, and their conduct during the battle of the 14th, that, bad as it had been, it had not seriously affected their fighting spirit as a whole, and this raises the interesting question:"Does an incompetent Staff demoralize an Army, or vice versa?" The two invariably act and react upon one another, but the consequences are rarely so acutely marked as in the present instance.

It is clear that the Prussian Army had lost but little of its fighting value when it came into actual contact with the enemy, but it seems equally clear from the testimony of many eye-witnesses, recorded in diaries and private letters, that the Staff, accustomed to the faultless routine discipline of the manoeuvre ground and the barrack yard, had already lost confidence in the men, owing to the ignorance these had displayed in ordinary outpost duties, the irregularities of the retreat from Schleitz and Saalfeld, and so forth.

Actually the marching discipline in the French Army was at least as bad as in the Prussian, probably worse, for the men straggled terribly and fell out by hundreds, whilst the Staff was at least as fertile in "orders and counter-orders" as that of their opponents; but neither for a moment lost confidence in one another, simply because they were all veterans together and had seen things immeasurably worse in previous campaigns, which, nevertheless, had ended victoriously. They certainly escaped the trial of an enforced retreat, but even had that trial arisen, they would have taken it as all in the day's work, for it was an essential part of the knowledge they had gained during the previous years of fighting, that the General had an absolute right to sacrifice any one fraction[1] of his Army in order to gain time for the remainder to execute the movements necessary for his desired combination; and knowing this, the sound of distant firing and the sight of a few wounded stragglers would not have affected their nerves in the slightest degree.

But in the Prussian Army all was different. When the senior officers had been the rounds of the outposts and found some facing the wrong way, and others hugging the detachments they were meant to protect, there was doubtless a great deal of heated language and difference of opinion, evident enough to the rank and file; consequently both began to distrust each other, as invariably happens on such occasions. Both probably reasoned that if things were already so bad, even before the enemy was in sight, what would it be when the bullets actually began to fly? and since each Regiment naturally believed itself no worse than another as soon as the distant boom of the guns was heard, imagination began to run riot, and it needed only the sight of a few wounded stragglers to precipitate a panic. The same men would have been steady enough once the plunge into action had been taken, as indeed they proved themselves to be, but they could not bear the imaginary punishment of others, because collectively they had never been taught to realize the inevitable consequences of any hostile collision.

This opens up a difficult problem, which most commanders, in time of peace, endeavour to shirk. How is one to bring home

---

1. Of course the defeated fraction must not be too large a portion of the whole.

to the men the crude fact that they are after all only counters with which the superior Commander *buys the time and information* he requires for his ulterior purposes, without shaking their "moral." It is of little use telling them of the losses the Regiment has borne in the past, for words make no impression at all in matters of this kind upon the average man, and practising attacks with casualties introduced is not of much avail because there is no resulting disorder. Even when disorder arises, as it often does when battalions are allowed to intermingle in the fighting line, the total absence of any real excitement or of danger gives no genuine opportunity for the officer to assert his individuality. The attempt to simulate an act which under fire would deserve the V.C. twice over, would simply expose the perpetrator to the derision of the whole command on a parade ground; and that is why such scenes, or the occasion for them, are instinctively avoided. This, however, is a digression which would lead one further than I have space to follow up; the point I wish to establish is only this, that practical strategy is far more influenced by the degree of mutual confidence between battalions and the General Staff than by all other factors put together. Yet this essential point is one which the conventional strategy of textbooks (in England at any rate) most consistently ignores, and I submit that this is the principal reason why War as a, whole is so little studied.

There is a strong racial strain in the average British officer of, say, ten years' service, developed by his school training and love of sport, that refuses to be caught by mere verbiage, however pedantically expressed, and insists on an answer which goes to the root of the matter.

This campaign, and this particular crisis of October 11, is a case in point.

Our books barely allude to this panic, and the average student with the map before him can never be brought to believe in the danger which threatened the Prussian Army until the full scope of the panic has been described to him.

How could Napoleon know that the Prussians would not concentrate their 98,000 men against such French troops as had already crossed to the left bank of the Saale on the morning of the 12th, and annihilate them even if they numbered 50,000 men? But until this new doctrine of the French General Staff appeared, no one could tell them that Napoleon had deliberately accepted this risk in principle, and was prepared to purchase the time necessary for the completion of his manoeuvre against the Prussian communications by the sacrifice of the two Corps of Lannes and Augereau if necessary. That, in fact, only Lannes was across the river seems to have been unknown to Napoleon, who, when he issued his orders on the night of the 11th-12th, had hardly made sufficient allowance for the delay in their delivery which actually arose, as pointed out above.

That the Prussian Headquarters' Staff were in ignorance of the positions actually held by the French on the night of the 11th-12th does not invalidate my argument, because in a friendly country they ought to have been thoroughly well informed. But Napoleon's resolution on this fateful night brings us face to face with the whole question of "the economy of force" in War which lay at the root of all his strategy and ultimately conditioned his methods.

Briefly it may be summed up as follows—"How much time can be bought at the price of so many thousand men," and the answer was based on current experience tempered by his own judgment.

This much Clausewitz saw clearly, but, curiously, he never reached forward to its complete application.

A Division, say of 10,000 men, could not be destroyed by the weapons and methods of the Armies with which he had served in less than six to eight hours, except of course under quite unusual conditions. An Army Corps could fairly be counted on to fight from daylight to darkness even against heavy odds. Two Corps might reasonably gain two days and one night by suitable manoeuvring in retreat. Hence, if the remainder of an Army, of say eight Corps, could be concentrated for battle within thirty-six hours, at the right time and place, all the conditions for success in the Napoleonic manoeuvre were fulfilled, and on these rough data all marches and dispositions were, in fact, arranged, and held good, until Napoleon invented the "case-shot" attack generally employed in his subsequent campaigns.

The essence however of this method lay in the possibility it contained of entirely vitiating these data by the sudden destruction of such covering bodies in perhaps half the time they were expected to resist. But Napoleon seems never to have realized that the "Linear" attack of Frederick's Infantry conferred upon the man who knew how to employ it exactly the same advantage.

Nothing in the Emperor's own experience, or that of his Generals, even suggested the possibility of such a rapid decision, because since Frederick the Great's day no one had ever been found to apply the idea of the "line" in the full simplicity with which he invariably conceived it. But that the idea in itself was capable of realization had been shown by Lord Lake in India[1] repeatedly, and was about to be proved by the British Infantry at Maida and in the Peninsula (at Salamanca particularly). For the sake of clearness let me recapitulate again in briefest form what the expression the "Linear" Tactics of Frederick really covered.

It had nothing to do with the advance of one or more battalions, or even brigades in deployed lines, but implied the sudden onslaught of a whole Corps at least, in deployed lines if practicable, but in any case with every available musket in the firing line and *no reserves behind it*; for if all went well, and the weight of metal thrown swept away all resist-

1. The reader should consult Col. Pearse's admirable *Life and Letters of Lord Lake,* from which it is quite clear that Lake, either consciously or unconsciously, had grasped for himself the Napoleonic doctrines.

ance, there would remain nothing for the reserves to accomplish. Cavalry alone would suffice to keep the beaten enemy on the run. No man was thus passively exposed to danger, and the risk to all was diminished to the utmost by the shortening of the time of exposure.

Now imagine Wellington, with even 50,000 men, watching his opportunity from the Landgrafenberg against Lannes and Augereau combined, and seizing it, as he seized it at Salamanca. Marmont's Army was defeated in less than three hours, would his comrades have escaped any better? If not, then what would have become of Napoleon's time calculation?

Herein lies the danger in the application of the Napoleonic strategic conception as a "normal" form, which it is certain to become by reason of its intrinsic simplicity before many years.

The ordinary General will seek to purchase "time" by the sacrifice of his men as Napoleon did, but without the latter's experience of war to guide him in such expenditure. Substantially the resisting power of a given unit is calculated generally, as in Napoleon's day, quite irrespective of the changes in war material which the century has brought, and indeed the teaching of recent campaigns, superficially considered, is held to have demonstrated an increase in the "retaining" power of a given unit rather than the contrary.

Now suppose a General were to arise who has seen that this gain in "retaining" power of modern troops arises not from the nature of their armament but from the topographical conditions under which they have been employed (the relative roadlessness of Bulgaria, South Africa, Manchuria, for instance), and with highly disciplined troops to apply this knowledge in Western Europe, and follow out the consequences.

I saw such an application of this idea made in the German manoeuvres of 1891, near Mühlhausen in Hanover, and the impression has never left me. Two Corps, the IV and XI, had gained touch of one another during the preceding operations, and their Cavalry Divisions had drawn off to the flanks;

that of the XI Corps being numerically much the stronger. The IV Corps began its advance next morning in the normal deployed formation, ready to fight at a moment's notice, skirmishers, supports, main body, reserve, and so forth.

From a plateau to the eastward two parallel ridges some 4,000 yards apart, extended for about three miles towards the plains, and a small brook marked by clumps of willows showed the drainage channel; the slopes of the ridges were very easy, slightly convex, and the ground was good going everywhere.

About 10 a.m. the skirmishers of the IV Corps were exchanging shots with a few riflemen of the XI Corps hidden amongst the willows, and behind them the whole IV Corps, or at least a great part of it, lay blocked out on the slope as shown in the sketch—

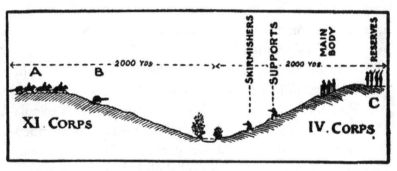

Suddenly, from my position, almost in prolongation of the valley, I saw the whole Corps Artillery of the Hessians[1] (18 batteries in all) dash over the brow of the hill at *A* and gallop forward to the break in the slope at *B*, where it unlimbered and at once opened a most rapid fire: no "ranging" was necessary against such a target. Then from the plateau to the eastward descended a perfect avalanche of horsemen (45 squadrons) which struck the IV Corps in flank, rode down between its several lines, and for some minutes the resulting confusion was indescribable. Then the "cease fire" sounded, and the officers rode up for the umpire's decision, which was

1. XI Corps is furnished by the Hessians.

so completely in favour of the success of the Cavalry charges, that operations ceased for the day and the troops were at once marched back to their night quarters.

Umpires' decisions are not always accepted by all parties, but in this instance I heard no dissentient voices during many subsequent discussions; even the Infantry, supposed to have been ridden over, amongst whom I had several friends, admitted their complete discomfiture. But even assuming the Cavalry to have been ultimately repulsed, it is quite clear that the confusion engendered by this combined Artillery and Cavalry surprise would have left the Infantry of the IV Corps completely at the mercy of the Hessians, who having no longer any aimed fire to fear, could have advanced at once in ordinary deployed lines and swept their adversaries away by magazine fire, precisely as the old British line with its volley firing and bayonets had so often done in India and the Peninsula, against a similarly disorganized enemy.

The whole IV Corps would have been destroyed as a fighting body, certainly within a couple of hours, and now note how this destruction would have affected the time calculations of the Army Commander, who had based his manoeuvre upon the endurance of this particular link in his chain. The initiative would have passed definitely to his adversary, and his remaining units would either have had to be recalled, or subjected to the risk of defeat in detail.

In the above instance, the Commander of the IV Corps may be regarded as an agent for the Commander-in-Chief sent out to *buy time,* in which operation he failed, because he encountered tactics for which his training had not prepared him, but it is not easy to see what others he could have employed.

Entrenching himself on or behind his own ridge *(G),* a proceeding probably precluded by his orders, would not have assisted him unless his adversary had been under imperative orders to attack him, which of course he could not be aware of with any degree of certainty. His enemy with his superiority in Cavalry would soon have felt out that he was immobilizing himself, and leaving only a few troops to observe the position, would have marched off with the remainder of his force to join his own Commander-in-Chief in an offensive on some other column. Moreover, as between troops of equal armament, the offensive is in itself the best method of gaining time because it compels the enemy's attention and magnifies his danger by the concealment the forward movement ensures.[1] Instinctively the defender feels that his enemy would not come on so boldly unless he had a strong force behind him, yet he hesitates to be bluffed out of his position by what may prove to be a mere screen of men, and his hesitation loses him the opportunity of beginning a timely retreat. This is an operation, by the way, which is only practicable with war-experienced, troops of very high quality, and therefore is one that is not at all likely to be undertaken hastily by any modern Commander at the head of modern peace-trained troops. Thus in the instance under discussion the Commander of the IV Corps had no alternative but to attack; yet on that particular ground, attack exposed him to certain annihilation unless he modified his tactics, an almost impossible undertaking in any Army in which a "normal" form of attack has once been allowed to take root.

He could have escaped this difficulty had it been possible for him to crown each successive ridge across his path by a line of batteries, ready to open fire the moment his enemy attempted to unlimber against him, but neither he nor any one else would have cared then, or would care now, to risk long lines of guns so far to the front in presence of the marked superiority in charging Cavalry which he knew his enemy to possess. This is where an Infantry trained to manoeuvre in the old Frederickian manner in long lines (either of company columns or deployed companies does

---

1. Compare Alvensleben's action with the III Corps at Vionville, 16/8/1870, and read in his life his own appreciation of the situation.

not signify), finds its opportunity, the essence of the idea being *the endurance of punishment without retaliation in kind*— the hardest of all ideas to instil into a peace-trained soldier's mind, but one which our pre-breach-loader experience (even as recently as in the Mutiny) has shown to be well within the capabilities of our seven-year service men, liberally stiffened by reservists and a reasonable proportion of re-engaged men.[1] With such men, and such a spirit, it would have been quite feasible for the Commander of the IV Corps to have gone back to the old "Linear" idea, and covered by a screen of real light troops (such as used to be furnished by the Old Light Division skirmishers at 12 paces interval), the Corps could have followed in two deployed lines 1,000 yards apart, so that practically each line would have had to be "ranged" upon separately, and the whole could not have been caught by the sweep of a single shrapnel shell without altering the fuses.

With such troops immediately at hand, the Artillery could have gone forward without fear of the Cavalry, and remained always available for immediate action if required.[2]

Against such troops, moreover, the Commander of the XI Corps would hardly have ventured upon the singularly bold method he actually adopted, for his guns would have been lost had the Infantry of the IV Corps once passed the line of the brook and the willows, for the slight convexity of the slopes prevented the Artillery from sweeping the ground right up to their muzzles, and this will be found to be almost invariably the case in all districts in the north of Europe likely to become the scene of any future decisive encounters.

---

1. In the time of the Mutiny the average length of service of the men in our Regiments was probably not nearly as high, as the death-rate (60 per mille), and the number of men invalided kept the proportion of older men with the colours very low indeed.

2. But this implies that the batteries have been trained to long advances in line at the gallop, by whole Brigades at least. In this instance the whole 18 batteries galloped forward together.

For the XI Corps to withdraw its Artillery would have been practically to commence a retreat, for its Infantry alone could never have advanced unsupported by guns down the slopes of the hill in face of the combined Infantry and Artillery fire from the other side of the hollow.

The only way open to the XI Corps to avert defeat would have been a counter-attack with the bayonet in old Peninsular style at the moment the enemy reached the brow of the hill and masked his own guns; but this again involves training on the old "Line" system, so that by whatever way one approaches the problem one is driven back to the ideal of the "line" as its ultimate solution, provided always that the men are good enough to stand the strain, and this solution is seen to be inevitable when we recall what has been proved above, *viz., that the essence of the "Line" conception was the economy of force resulting from obtaining the greatest possible development of fire with the least useless exposure of men.* Where the old British system exposed but 15,000 men to the square mile the French method would have exposed up to 70,000, and since fully nine-tenths of the hits in a general action are caused by bullets striking targets at which they were not deliberately aimed, it is clear that for an equal volume of bullets delivered, the 15,000 men would catch fewer than the 70,000.

The only question that remains is whether it is possible to train men nowadays to stand up to fire as they did in the past? and the answer is another question, "Why not?" It does not hurt more to be killed by a bullet to-day than two centuries ago, and all history shows that the actual risk of being hit in a given unit of time is very much lower than it formerly was.[1]

---

1. In the period before the French Revolution, a man's life (or limb) in battle was hardly worth thirty-six hours' purchase, i.e., an Insurance Company would have lost on such a deal. In the first decade of the Revolution fortunes could have been made on these terms and the same would have been the case in Manchuria.

The psychological fact remains, that in moments of intense excitement all except the very strongest characters cease to act or think as free agents, but are absolutely dominated by the resultant will-power of the "crowd" to which they for the moment belong, and this "resultant" will-power of the mass will always revert to the primitive instinct of the race.

This instinct may for a time be overlaid by an acquired intellectual habit—in other words, you may teach a man by appealing to his reason to lie down behind cover, and for a time he may excel in the practice, as did the Boers, but when the danger really becomes imminent the instinct reasserts itself, and troops belonging to any race possessing anything approaching to a fighting tradition, will always stand up to meet a charge before the lower form of instinct for self-preservation triumphs for good and all.

White men will not accept death lying down, and the object of all drill-training should be to utilize this instinct of aggression, and not to work against it, by trying to place self-preservation in the foremost place.

This mistake the old drill books never made; the skirmishers (war-selected men) never worked in mobs amenable to the crowd impulse; but in the "line" everything was sacrificed to create an overwhelming impulse to go forward; and so strongly was this willpower of the closed formation developed, that not even a drummer boy was allowed to duck to a passing round shot after the second time.

Even the unarmed drivers of the Artillery were expected to sit quietly at attention on their horses for hours under a heavy fire, and this tradition remained with us throughout the old long-service days. It held good even in the Navy, where sometimes a vessel fought an action within forty-eight hours of leaving port with a raw crew, perhaps one-half of which had been pressed during the week before sailing. Yet even middies and powder monkeys of thirteen to fourteen years of age conformed heroically to the accepted standard.

During the sixties and seventies of the last century, the war-seasoned soldiers of Europe who had seen British troops under fire, found no words strong enough to convey their praise of them. At the storming of the Pei-ho Forts, when the French and British were advancing side by side under a heavy fire, the former were laughing, joking and ducking to the round shot as they flew over them, but the British Regiment (the 68th I believe) went forward without a sound or a quiver, and the French Commander who had seen service in Algiers, the Crimea, and Italy, turned round to his British colleagues and said that now he understood the secret of past British victories. "Our men," he explained, "are doing quite as well as usual, but they never will or can emulate the performance of their British comrades" (or words to that effect). During the same Campaign we still used time fuses for shrapnel shell, which could be set for several ranges by boring; essentially the same as we had used in the Peninsula. The French time fuse could only be set for two ranges, and the French explained this by saying that it was all very well for such men as ours, they could be trusted not to get excited, but that it would be impossible for them to put implements requiring such deliberate treatment in the hands of their own troops. The Prussians went even further, for they rejected shrapnel altogether, as requiring more than they could expect from the average of their rank and file.

If this spirit existed only forty years ago, and there are hundreds of eye-witnesses still amongst us to prove that in well-disciplined units it lasted even longer, it is certain that it is still at hand ready when we find the Leader who will know how to evoke it, for the instincts of a race are the growth of centuries and cannot be extinguished by any education, however drastic, in a single generation. If many men brought back from the fields of South Africa a different impression, that was only because circumstances after the first few weeks never allowed the troops a fair chance. That it was there was proved by the attack of Penn Symon's Brigade, at Talana Hill, the Devonshires in Ladysmith, the Guards and the Marines at Belmont and Graspan. Probably no finer feat of arms has ever been witnessed in history than the advance of the Guards at the former place, extended at 4 paces without checking to fire a shot. For such men, backed up by following lines, nothing was impossible; but from that period onward neither the circumstances or the ground rendered a decisive attack feasible in the modern European style, and the fact that we never made one cannot be taken as proofs that the spirit to carry one through was wanting. But our next great fighting is not likely to be against Boer tactics, or in a country even remotely resembling their territory. Wherever it may be we shall have to deal with the Napoleonic conception of battle, and to meet troops trained in the spirit of the Revolutionary levies, and our best means to encounter these successfully will be to study the spirit of our own institutions and realize how we came to reap the gratitude of Europe by our final victory at Waterloo, and when we have done so, let us not forget that it was to the despised and rejected pedants and drill-masters of Prussia that we owed the fundamental principles on which our own victories were based.

The tactics of Frederick the Great perished on the field of Jena through no fault of their own, and the contumely and scorn so lavishly poured upon the old Prussian Army by the generations which have since elapsed are entirely unmerited. The Army fell from one cause only, *viz.*, that its leaders had mistaken the spirit of the age, and therefore shunned the responsibility of great resolutions, and that is the one and lasting lesson the campaign has to teach us. To conquer there must be a man to "will," and men will never dare to "will" until they have learnt the inherent truth contained in Scharnhorst's saying, "In War it is not so much what one does that matters, as the fact that one does something at once, and does it thoroughly."

It would lead me far beyond the scope of the present study to describe in detail the ultimate break up and annihilation of the Prussian Armies; but to all who wish to profit vicariously by the lessons of defeat, I would most earnestly recommend the study of Von der Goltz's work, *Von Jena bis zu Preussische's Eylau.*

We cannot hope to carry the flood-tide of victory always with us, but we shall be fortunate indeed if when the dark days come upon us we can find men who have steeled their characters to know the worst that war can bring, and like the regenerators of Prussia, will pursue the path of Duty.

"Durch Nacht, und Blut, zur Licht."[1]

---

1. "Through Night and Blood to Light,"—the interpretation of the German colours: black, red, white.

LEONAUR

ALSO FROM LEONAUR

AVAILABLE IN SOFTCOVER OR HARDCOVER WITH DUST JACKET

THE COMPLEAT RIFLEMAN HARRIS *by Benjamin Harris as told to & transcribed by Captain Henry Curling*—The adventures of a soldier of the 95th (Rifles) during the Peninsular Campaign of the Napoleonic Wars

WITH WELLINGTON'S LIGHT CAVALRY *by William Tomkinson*—The Experiences of an officer of the 16th Light Dragoons in the Peninsular and Waterloo campaigns of the Napoleonic Wars.

SERGEANT BOURGOGNE *by Adrien Bourgogne*—With Napoleon's Imperial Guard in the Russian Campaign and on the Retreat from Moscow 1812 - 13.

SWORDS OF HONOUR *by Henry Newbolt & Stanley L. Wood*—The Careers of Six Outstanding Officers from the Napoleonic Wars, the Wars for India and the American Civil War, with dozens of illustrations by Stanley L. Wood.

SURTEES OF THE RIFLES *by William Surtees*—A Soldier of the 95th (Rifles) in the Peninsular campaign of the Napoleonic Wars.

ENSIGN BELL IN THE PENINSULAR WAR *by George Bell*—The Experiences of a young British Soldier of the 34th Regiment 'The Cumberland Gentlemen' in the Napoleonic wars.

HUSSAR IN WINTER *by Alexander Gordon*—A British Cavalry Officer during the retreat to Corunna in the Peninsular campaign of the Napoleonic Wars.

NAPOLEONIC WAR STORIES *by Sir Arthur Quiller-Couch*—Tales of soldiers, spies, battles & sieges from the Peninsular & Waterloo campaingns.

JOURNALS OF ROBERT ROGERS OF THE RANGERS *by Robert Rogers*—The exploits of Rogers & the Rangers in his own words during 1755-1761 in the French & Indian War.

KERSHAW'S BRIGADE VOLUME 1 *by D. Augustus Dickert*—Manassas, Seven Pines, Sharpsburg (Antietam), Fredricksburg, Chancellorsville, Gettysburg, Chickamauga, Chattanooga, Fort Sanders & Bean Station..

KERSHAW'S BRIGADE VOLUME 2 *by D. Augustus Dickert*—At the wilderness, Cold Harbour, Petersburg, The Shenandoah Valley and Cedar Creek.

A TIGER ON HORSEBACK *by L. March Phillips*—The Experiences of a Trooper & Officer of Rimington's Guides - The Tigers - during the Anglo-Boer war 1899 - 1902.

Printed in the USA
CPSIA information can be obtained
at www.ICGtesting.com
LVHW092255011123
762562LV00032B/946/J